8

american popular piano

ETUDES

Compositions by
Christopher Norton

Additional Compositions and Arrangements
Dr. Scott McBride Smith

Editor
Dr. Scott McBride Smith

Associate Editor
Clarke MacIntosh

Book Design & Engraving
Andrew Jones

Cover Design
Wagner Design

A Note about this Book

Pop music styles can be grouped into three broad categories:

- **lyrical** — pieces with a beautiful singing quality and rich harmonies; usually played at a slow tempo;
- **rhythmic** — more up-tempo pieces, with energetic, catchy rhythms; these often have a driving left hand part;
- **ensemble** — works meant to be played with other musicians, or with backing tracks (or both!); this type of piece requires careful listening and shared energy.

American Popular Piano has been deliberately designed to develop skills in all three areas.

You can integrate the cool, motivating pieces in **American Popular Piano** into your piano studies in several ways.

- pick a piece you like and learn it; when you're done, pick another!
- choose a piece from each category to develop a complete range of skills in your playing;
- polish a particular favorite for your local festival or competition. Works from **American Popular Piano** are featured on the lists of required pieces for many festivals and competitions;
- use the pieces as optional contemporary selections in music examinations;
- Or...just have fun!

Going hand-in-hand with the repertoire in **American Popular Piano** are the innovative **Etudes Albums** and **Skills Books**, designed to enhance each student's musical experience by building technical and aural skills.

- **Technical Etudes** in both Classical and Pop Styles are based on musical ideas and technical challenges drawn from the repertoire. Practice these to improve your chops!
- **Improvisation Etudes** offer an exciting new approach to improvisation that guides students effortlessly into spontaneous creativity. Not only does the user-friendly module structure integrate smoothly into traditional lessons, it opens up a whole new understanding of the repertoire being studied.
- **Skills Books** help students develop key supporting skills in sight-reading, ear-training and technique; presented in complementary study modules that are both practical and effective.

Use all of the elements of **American Popular Piano** together to incorporate a comprehensive course of study into your everyday routine. The carefully thought-out pacing makes learning almost effortless. Making music and real progress has never been so much fun!

Library and Archives Canada Cataloguing in Publication

Norton, Christopher, 1953-

American popular piano [music] : etudes / compositions by Christopher Norton ;
additional compositions and arrangements, Scott McBride Smith ;
editor, Scott McBride Smith ; associate editor, Clarke MacIntosh.

To be complete in 11 volumes.
Publisher's nos.: APP E-00 (Level P); APP E-01 (Level 1); APP E-02 (Level 2); APP E-03 (Level 3); APP E-04 (Level 4); APP E-05 (Level 5).
Contents: Level P -- Level 1 -- Level 2 -- Level 3 -- Level 4 -- Level 5.
Miscellaneous information: The series is organized in 11 levels, from preparatory to level 10, each including a repertoire album, an etudes album, a skills book, a "technic" book, and an instrumental backings compact disc.

ISBN 1-897379-11-0 (level P).--ISBN 1-897379-12-9 (level 1).--ISBN 1-897379-13-7 (level 2).--ISBN 1-897379-14-5 (level 3).--
ISBN 1-897379-15-3 (level 4).--ISBN 1-897379-16-1 (level 5).--ISBN 978-1-897379-11-0 (level P).--ISBN 978-1-897379-12-7 (level 1).--
ISBN 978-1-897379-13-4 (level 2).--ISBN 978-1-897379-14-1 (level 3).--ISBN 978-1-897379-15-8 (level 4).--ISBN 978-1-897379-16-5 (level 5).--
ISBN 978-1-897379-17-2 (level 6).--ISBN 978-1-897379-18-9 (level 7).--ISBN 978-1-897379-19-6 (level 8)

1. Piano--Studies and exercises. I. Smith, Scott McBride II. MacIntosh, S. Clarke, 1959- III. Title. IV. Title: Études

MT222.N884 2006 **786.2** **C2006-906214-5**

LEVEL 8 ETUDES

Table of Contents

Improv Etude - Barbican Blues

Module 1

Concept: Dominant 7 chords

A **Dominant 7 chord** (also known as a 7 chord) combines a major triad (e.g., D-F♯-A) with a minor 7th above the root (e.g., C). Sometimes this is done using all four notes (e.g., D-F♯-A-C), but often it is done with only three notes to achieve the same sound.

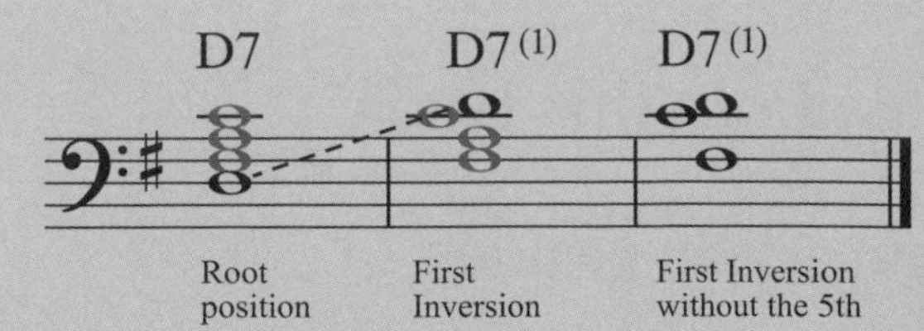

7 chords may be written in **first inversion**. In a first inversion 7 chord, the third of the chord is on the bottom. One way to change a root position 7 chord to first inversion is to take the root off the bottom and put it on top. When only three notes are used to play a first inversion 7 chord, it is usual to omit the 5th of the chord.

A Label the first inversion 7 chords with their lettername (e.g., D7 or E7) and a bracketed 1 for "first inversion". Practice the left hand first *without*, then *with* the backing track.

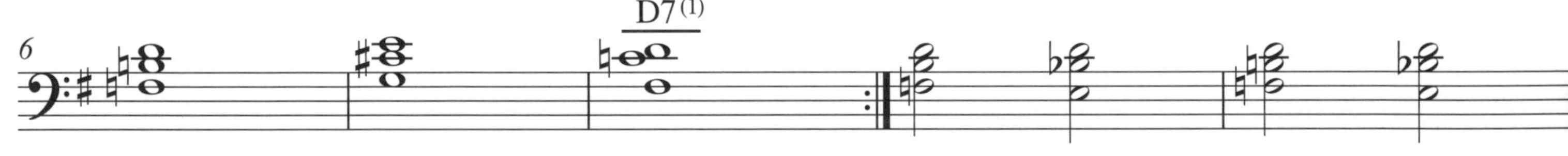

B Tap this rhythm while counting out loud; repeat until memorized. Then tap the rhythm with your right hand while playing the chord progression with your left. Finally, make up your own rhythms to go with the left hand chord progression.

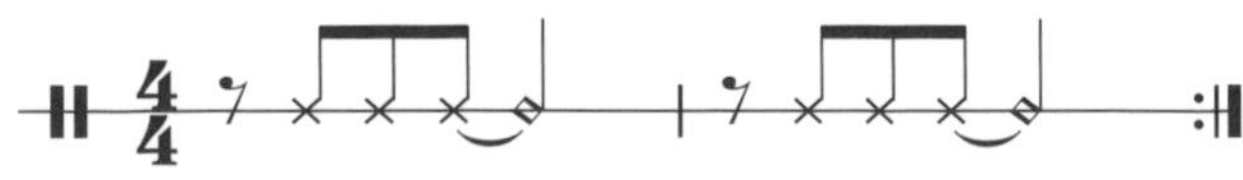

Improv Tools

To improvise on *Barbican Blues*, you will use two different sets of Improv Notes: one based on the **G Blues scale**, the other based on the **A Blues scale**.

One way to describe the **Blues scale** is as a **minor pentatonic** with an added lowered 5th scale degree. In this way, the **G Blues scale** would be described as a G **minor pentatonic** (G, B♭, C, D, F♮) with an added lowered 5th scale degree (D♭).

G Blues scale

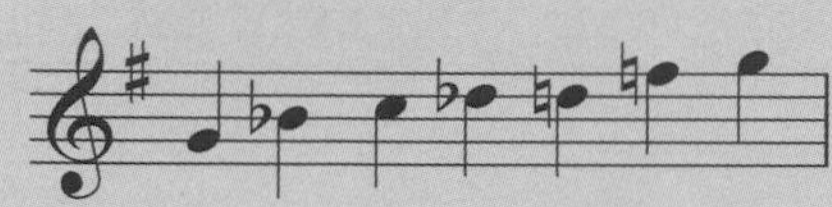

Here are two Improv Tools you can use to make your scale-based improvisation interesting and musical.

Rhythmic Shift: play an idea and then repeat it starting on a different beat:

Grace Notes: liven up your improvisation with grace notes:

C Using the Improv Notes Set A or B as indicated in the score, play various right hand improvisations. Use the Improv Tools, above, to get started. Practice *with* the backing track.

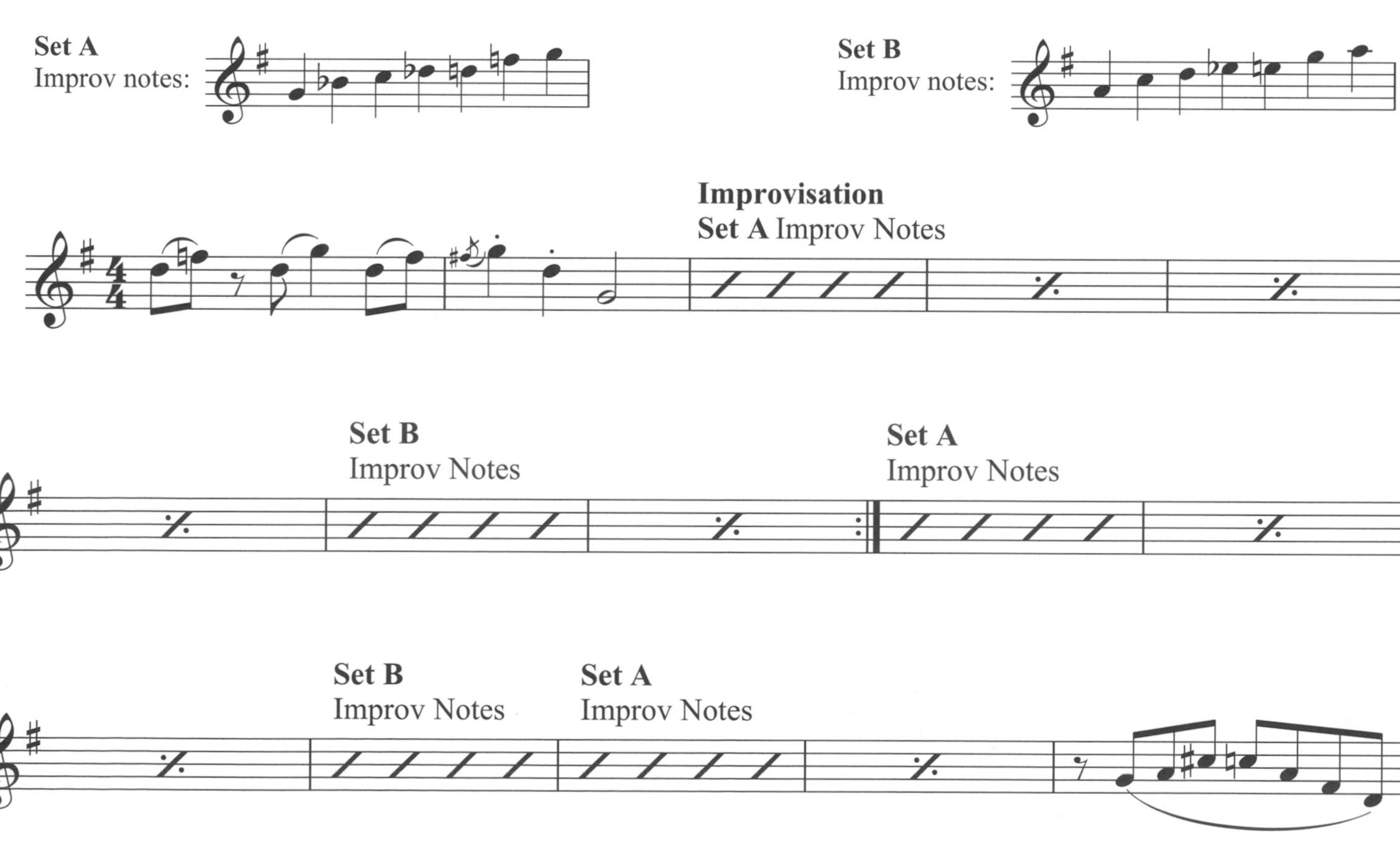

D Now improvise hands together. Practice first *without*, then *with* the backing track.

✔ **Improv Tip:** *In a swing piece like Barbican Blues, keep your improvised melodies relaxed and melodic.*

Vamping Tools

Vamping is an improvised accompaniment style. It often features repeated patterns based on blocked chords or broken chords in the right hand against single notes in the left hand.

You can vary right hand chords in several ways:
Vamp Idea 1 – play a repeated rhythmic pattern:

Idea 2 – all "on-beat" chords:

Idea 3 – a combination of on-beat and rhythm pattern chords:

E Vamp various right hand accompaniments using the chords [in brackets] indicated below. Use the Vamping Tools, above, to get started. Practice first *without*, then *with* the backing track.

6 D7(1)

11 D7(1) D7(1)

16 E7(1) D7(1) E7(1) D7(1)

Improv Etude - Barbican Blues

Module 2

Concept: Dominant 7 chords

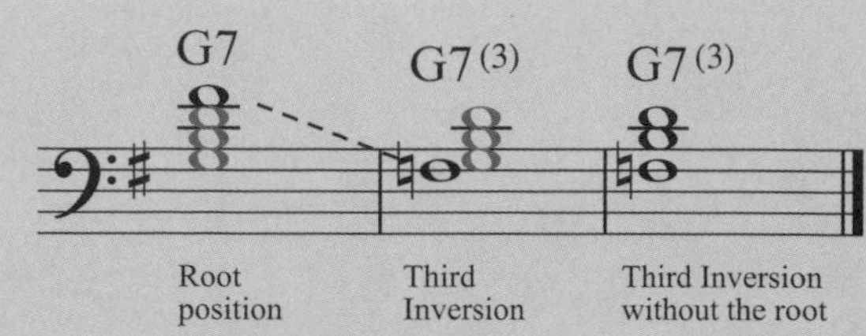

A **Dominant 7 chord** (also known as a 7 chord) combines a major triad (e.g., G-B-D) with a minor 7th above the root (e.g., F♮). Sometimes this is done using all four notes (e.g., G-B-D-F♮), but often it is done with only three notes to achieve the same sound.

7 chords may be written in **third inversion**. In a third inversion 7 chord, the minor seventh of the chord is on the bottom. One way to change a root position 7 chord to third inversion is to take the 7th off the top and put it on the bottom. When only three notes are used to play a third inversion 7 chord, it is usual to omit the root.

A Label the third inversion 7 chords with their lettername (e.g., G7 or A7) and a bracketed 3 for "third inversion". Practice the left hand first *without*, then *with* the backing track.

G7(3)

6 D7(1)

11 D7(1) D7(1)

16 E7(1) D7(1) E7(1) D7(1)

B Tap this rhythm while counting out loud; repeat until memorized. Then tap the rhythm with your right hand while playing the chord progression with your left. Finally, make up your own rhythms to go with the left hand chord progression.

Improv Tools

Idea & Variation is another Improv Tool you can use, as well as **Rhythmic Shift** and **Grace Notes**.

Improvisations can also use arpeggio-based ideas.

Rhythmic Shift: play an idea and then repeat it starting on a different beat:

Grace Notes: can be particularly effective for the style of a "blues" piece:

Idea & Variation: play an idea and then repeat it with a slight variation:

C Using the Improv Notes Set A or B as indicated in the score, play various right hand improvisations. Use the Improv Tools, above and in the previous Module, to get started. Practice *with* the backing track.

Set A
Improv notes:

Set B
Improv notes:

Improvisation
Set A Improv Notes

6

Set B
Improv Notes

Set A
Improv Notes

11

Set B
Improv Notes

Set A
Improv Notes

16

D Now improvise hands together. Practice first *without*, then *with* the backing track.

✔ **Improv Tip:** *A Rhythmic Shift will work particularly well when the chord progression stays the same for two bars or more.*

Vamping Tools

Vamps can also use broken chords in the right hand. You can create interest by varying the starting note of the arpeggio.

Vamp Idea 1 – start from the bottom note of the chord:

Idea 2 – start from the top note of the chord:

Idea 3 – start from the middle note of the chord:

E Vamp various right hand accompaniments using the chords [in brackets] indicated below. Use the Vamping Tools, above and in the previous Module, to get started. Practice first *without*, then *with* the backing track.

G7(3) G7(3) G7(3)

6 G7(3) A7(3) D7(1) G7(3) G7(3)

11 G7(3) A7(3) D7(1) G7(3) A7(3) D7(1)

16 G7(3) E7(1) A7(3) D7(1) G7(3) E7(1) A7(3) D7(1) G7(3)

Improv Etude - Barbican Blues

Module 3

Concept: 9 chords

A **9 chord** is a **7 chord** with the 9th scale degree added. Sometimes this is done using all five notes – a major triad (e.g., C-E-G) with the minor 7th (e.g., B♭) and major 9th (e.g., D) added (e.g., C-E-G-B♭-D) – or sometimes it is done with only three notes to achieve the same sound.

C9
C9 (1)
C9 (1)
Root position
First Inversion
First Inversion no Root or 5th

9 chords may be written in **first inversion**. In a first inversion 9 chord, the third of the chord is on the bottom. One way to change a root position 9 chord to first inversion is to take the root off the bottom and put it up an octave to be the second note from the top – just underneath the 9th.

For improvising on *Barbican Blues*, the 5th and root will be left out.

A Label the first inversion 9 chords with their lettername (e.g. C9) and a bracketed 1 for "first inversion". Practice the left hand first *without*, then *with* the backing track.

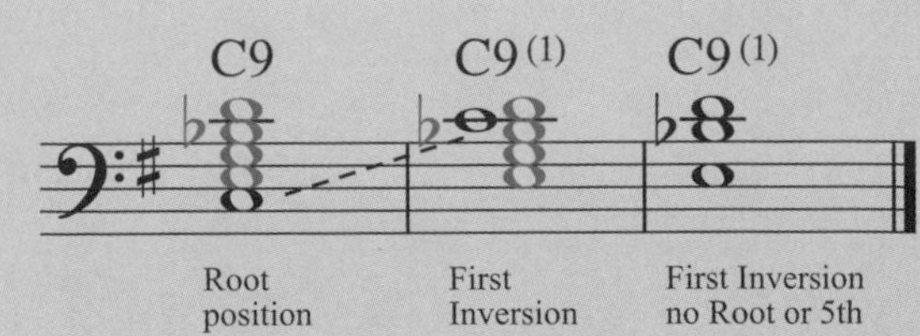

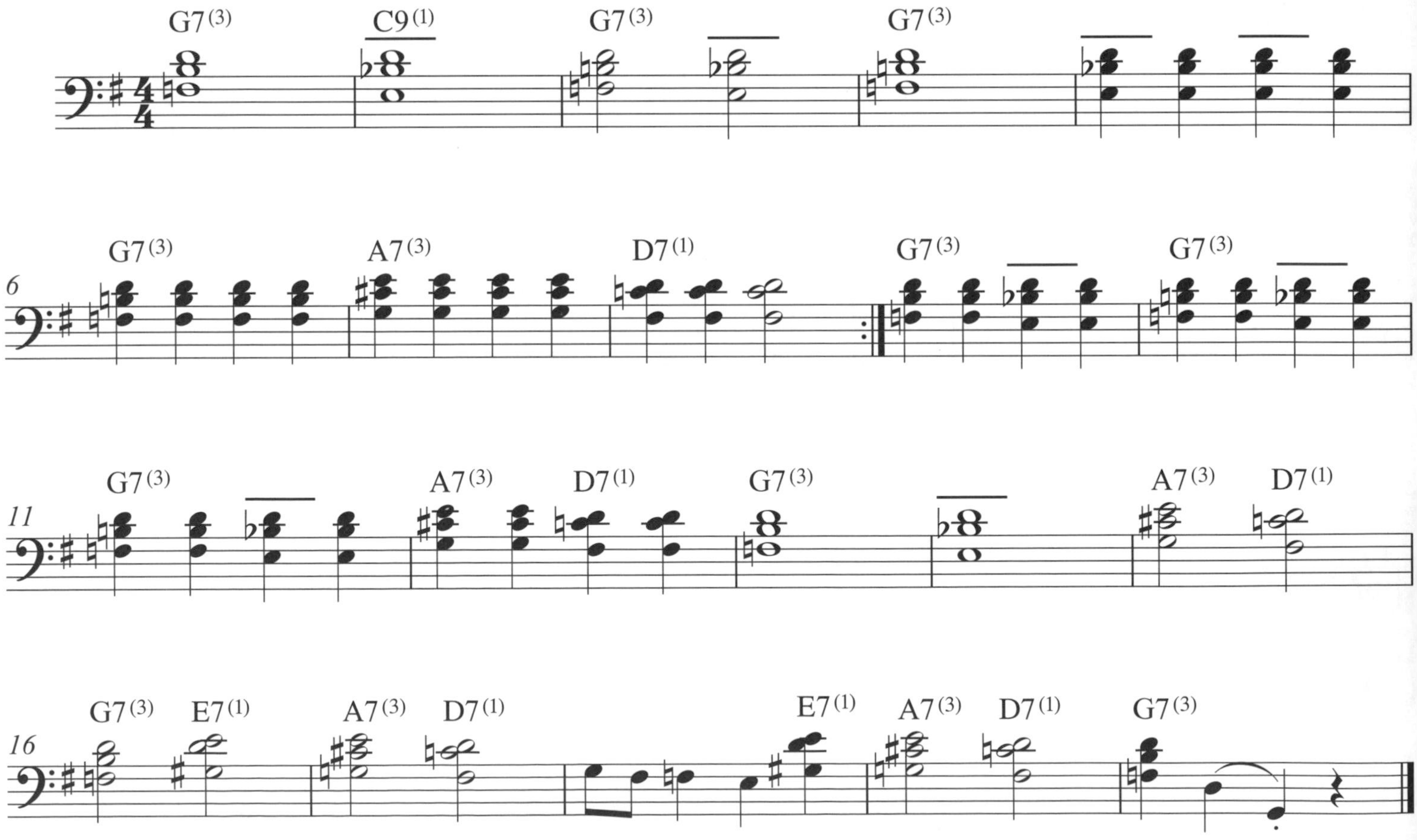

G7 (3)
C9 (1)
G7 (3)
G7 (3)
6
G7 (3)
A7 (3)
D7 (1)
G7 (3)
G7 (3)
11
G7 (3)
A7 (3)
D7 (1)
G7 (3)
A7 (3)
D7 (1)
16
G7 (3)
E7 (1)
A7 (3)
D7 (1)
E7 (1)
A7 (3)
D7 (1)
G7 (3)

B Tap this rhythm while counting out loud; repeat until memorized. Then tap the rhythm with your right hand while playing the chord progression with your left. Finally, make up your own rhythms to go with the left hand chord progression.

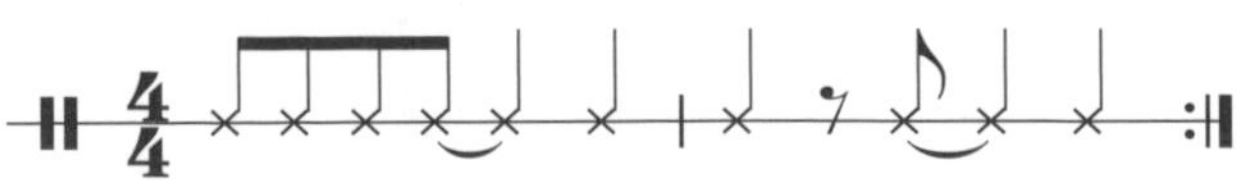

Improv Tools

There are other Improv Tools you can use to add color and interest to your improvisation. These Tools can be used with either scale-based or arpeggio-based ideas.

Direction Change: play an idea that changes direction to create contrast:

Tremolo: often used by blues players, experiment with playing them fast or slow to see which works for you:

Call and Response: play an idea, then "answer" it with a contrasting idea:

C Using the Improv Notes Set A or B as indicated in the score, play various right hand improvisations. Use the Improv Tools, above and in the previous Modules, to get started. Practice *with* the backing track.

Set A
Improv notes:

Set B
Improv notes:

Improvisation
Set A Improv Notes

6

Set B
Improv Notes

Set A
Improv Notes

11

Set B
Improv Notes

Set A
Improv Notes

16

D Now improvise hands together. Practice first *without*, then *with* the backing track.

✔ **Improv Tip:** *Keep left hand repeated quarter notes light, like a guitar strummed with the thumb.*

Vamping Tools

You can use a mix of blocked and broken chords in your vamp.

Vamp Idea 1 – an arpeggio followed by syncopated blocked chords:

Idea 2 – syncopated blocked chords followed by arpeggios:

Idea 3 – arpeggios followed by on-beat blocked chords:

E Vamp various right hand accompaniments using the chords [in brackets] indicated below. Use the Vamping Tools, above and in the previous Modules, to get started. Practice first *without*, then *with* the backing track.

G7(3) C9(1) G7(3) C9(1) G7(3) C9(1)

6 G7(3) A7(3) D7(1) G7(3) C9(1) G7(3) C9(1)

11 G7(3) C9(1) A7(3) D7(1) G7(3) C9(1) A7(3) D7(1)

16 G7(3) E7(1) A7(3) D7(1) G7(3) E7(1) A7(3) D7(1) G7(3)

Improv Etude - Sparkling

Module 1

Concept: second inversion

A triad is a three note chord. A **root position triad** in **close position** is written line-line-line or space-space-space. A chord takes its name from the bottom note of the chord in **root position**, called the **root**.

Chords may also be written in **second inversion**. A second inversion triad has the fifth of the chord on the bottom.

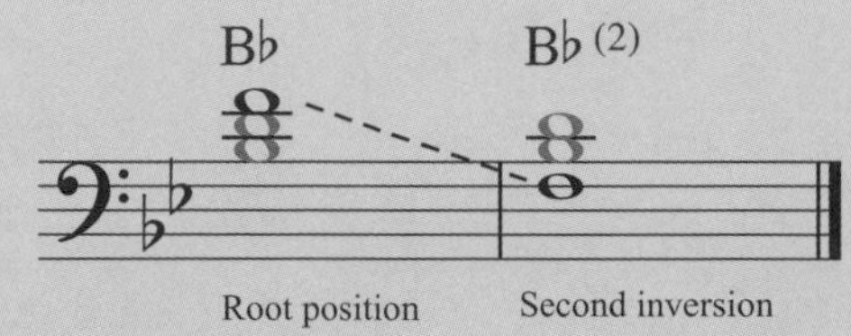

One way to change a root position triad to second inversion is to take the top note and move it to the bottom.

A Label the second inversion triads with their lettername and a bracketed 2 for "second inversion". Practice the left hand first *without*, then *with* the backing track.

B♭(2)

B Tap this rhythm while counting out loud; repeat until memorized. Then tap the rhythm with your right hand while playing the chord progression with your left. Finally, make up your own rhythms to go with the left hand chord progression.

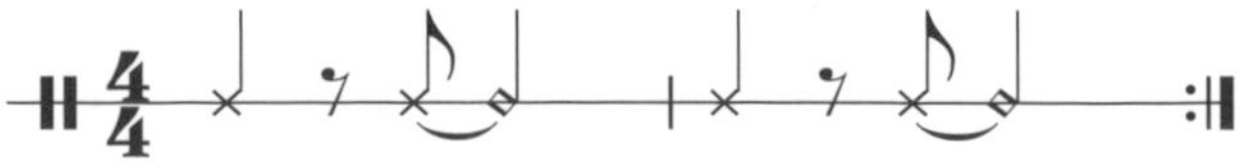

Improv Tools

Improvisations often use scale-based ideas. To improvise on *Sparkling*, you will use an Improv Notes Set based on the **B♭ major scale**.

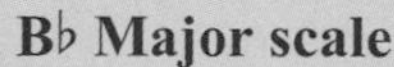

There are specific Improv Tools you can use to make your scale-based improvisation interesting and musical.

Idea & Variation: play a scale-based idea and then repeat it slightly varied (even by as little as one note!):

Call & Response: play an idea and then "answer" it with a contrasting idea:

C Using the Improv Notes Set as indicated in the score, play various right hand improvisations. Use the Improv Tools, above, to get started. Practice *with* the backing track.

D Now improvise hands together. Practice first *without*, then *with* the backing track.

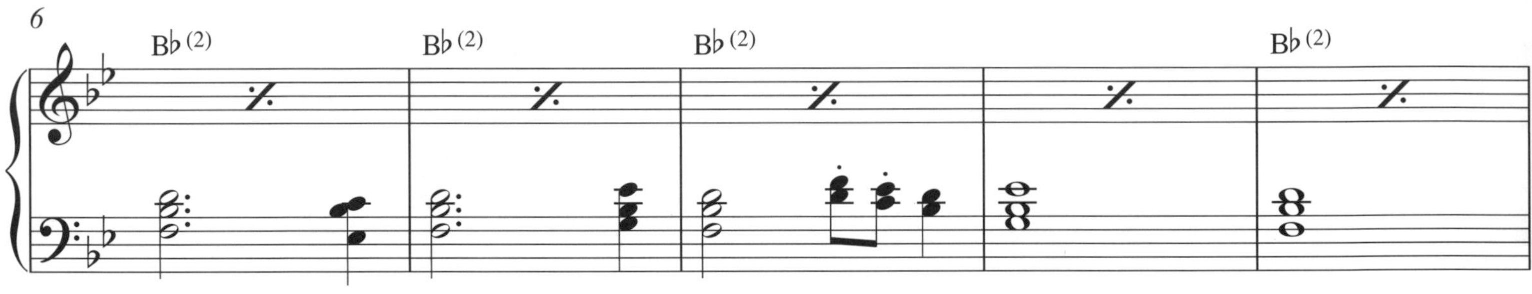

✔ **Improv Tip:** *Get your left hand really "tight" with the backing track before adding right hand ideas.*

Vamping Tools

Vamping is an improvised accompaniment style often featuring chords in the right hand against single notes in the left hand. When the left hand part is busy, such as the bass **riff** in *Sparkling*, the right hand can be simpler, using rhythmic patterns to create interest.

Vamp Idea 1 – blocked chords that sync with the left hand rhythm:

Idea 2 – a driving right hand "shot" followed by a dramatic rest:

Idea 3 – the right hand "shot" with blocked chords throughout:

E Vamp various right hand accompaniments using the chords [in brackets] indicated below. Use the Vamping Tools, above, to get started. Practice first *without*, then *with* the backing track.

Improv Etude - Sparkling

Module 2

Concept: first inversion & split chords

Remember that a triad is a three note chord. Triads may be written in **first inversion**. In a first inversion triad, the third of the chord is on the bottom. One way to change a root position triad to first inversion is to take the root off the bottom and put it on top.

Split chords can occur when playing chords with both hands. A split chord has a Bass note in the left hand that is not the root of the chord – sometimes it is not a note from the chord at all. The top chord of a split chord may be in first inversion.

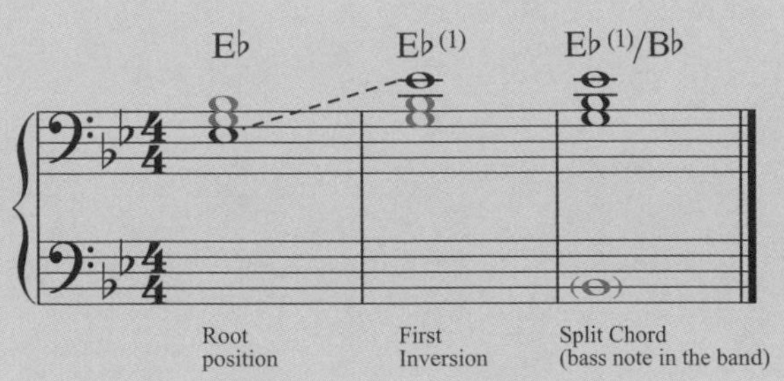

In the *Sparkling* improvisation, the "B♭" bass note is played in the backing track, creating a split chord sound in relation to the left hand chord.

A Label the first inversion triads and split chords with their lettername (E♭ or E♭/B♭) and a bracketed 1 to indicate "first inversion". Practice the left hand first *without*, then *with* the backing track.

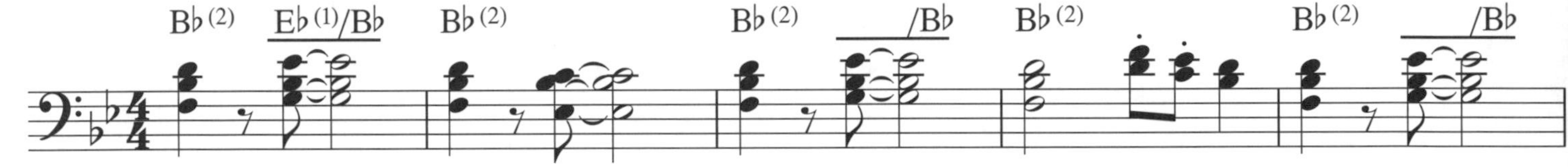

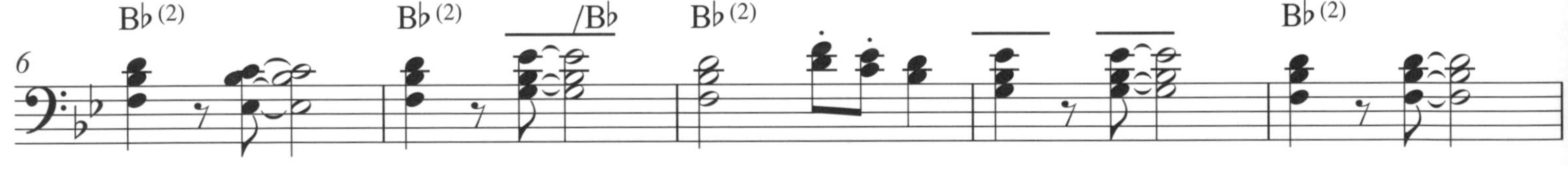

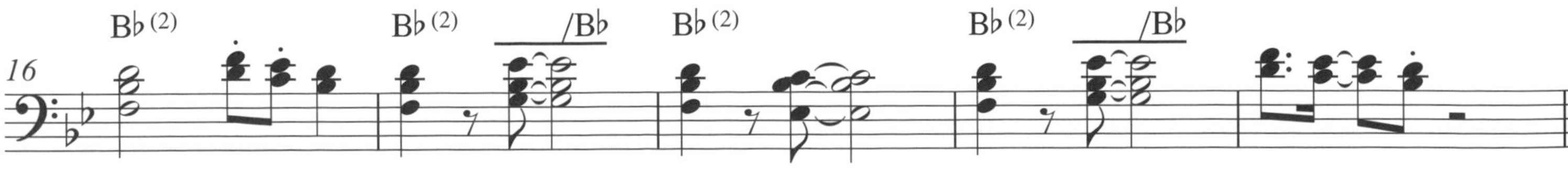

B Tap this rhythm while counting out loud; repeat until memorized. Then tap the rhythm with your right hand while playing the chord progression with your left. Finally, make up your own rhythms to go with the left hand chord progression.

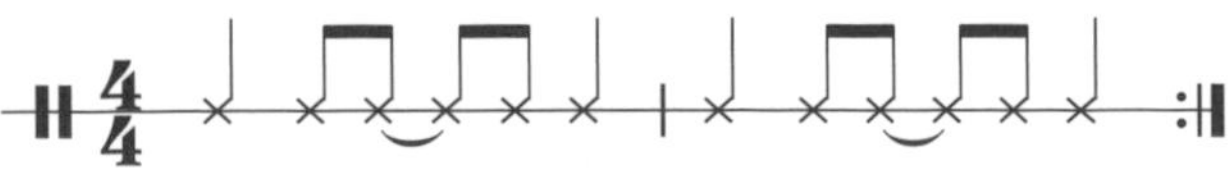

Improv Tools

Grace Notes is another Improv Tool you can use, in addition to the **Idea & Variation** and **Call & Response**.

Your improvisations can also use arpeggio-based ideas.

Idea & Variation: play an arpeggio-based idea and then repeat it with a slight variation:

Call & Response: play an idea and then "answer" it with a contrasting idea:

Grace Notes: add "drops" of interest to your improvisation with the occassional use of grace notes:

C Using the Improv Notes Set as indicated in the score, play various right hand improvisations. Use the Improv Tools, above and in the previous Module, to get started. Practice *with* the backing track.

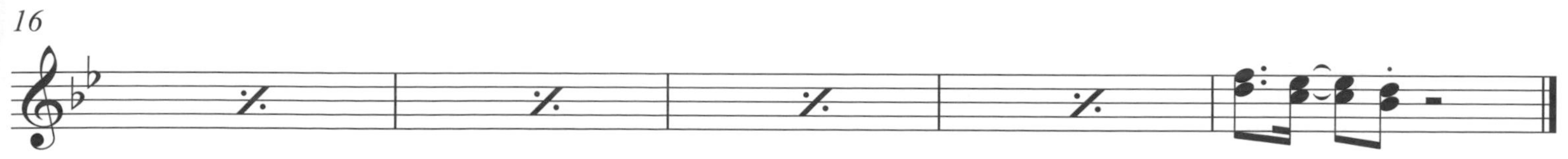

D Now improvise hands together. Practice first *without*, then *with* the backing track.

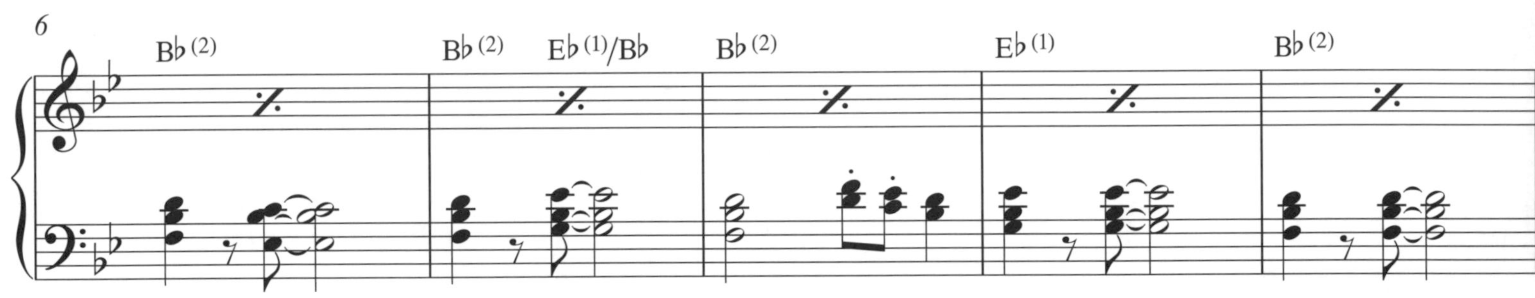

✔ **Improv Tip:** *Try creating contrast in your improvisation by alternating between busy sections, with many fast notes, and calmer sections, with longer held notes or rests.*

Vamping Tools

Your Vamp can also use broken chords in the right hand to create interest against the bass riff.

Vamp Idea 1: an arpeggio figure starting at the bottom:

Idea 2: an arpeggio figure that starts at the top:

Idea 3: start in the middle, then hint at blocked chords:

E Vamp various right hand accompaniments using the chords [in brackets] indicated below. Use the Vamping Tools, above and in the previous Module, to get started. Practice first *without*, then *with* the backing track.

Improv Etude - Sparkling

Module 3

Concept: sus4 chords

A suspension **sus4 chord** (also known as a **sus chord**), is created when the fourth degree of a scale is used in a chord instead of the third degree, "suspending" the resolution we expect to hear.

A suspension can be applied to any chord. To change a root position **7 chord** to a **7sus Chord**, take the third degree of the scale and move it up to the fourth degree. Just like 7 chords, 7sus chords may be written in **third inversion**.

F7
F7sus
F7sus (3)
F7sus (3)
Root position
Root position
Third Inversion
Third Inversion without the root

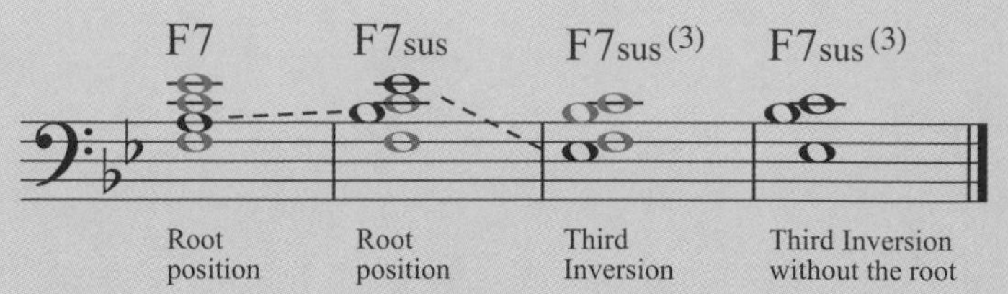

One way to change a root position 7sus chord to third inversion is to move the 7th from the top to the bottom.

For improvising on *Sparkling*, the root will be left out, using only three notes to achieve the same sound.

A Label the third inversion 7sus chords with their lettername (e.g., F7sus) and a bracketed 3 for "third inversion". Practice the left hand first *without*, then *with* the backing track.

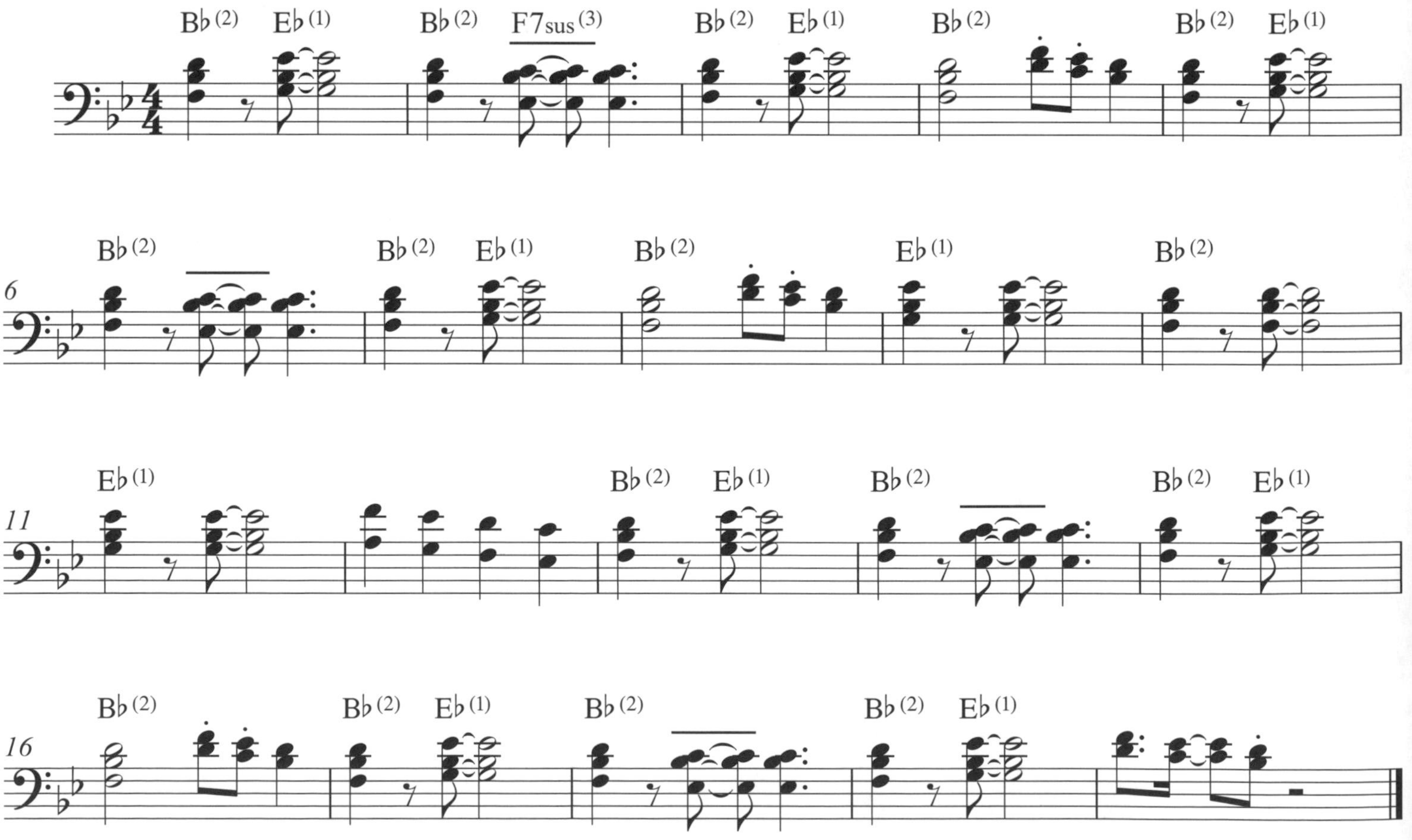

B♭(2) E♭(1) B♭(2) F7sus(3) B♭(2) E♭(1) B♭(2) B♭(2) E♭(1)
6
B♭(2) B♭(2) E♭(1) B♭(2) E♭(1) B♭(2)
11
E♭(1) B♭(2) E♭(1) B♭(2) B♭(2) E♭(1)
16
B♭(2) B♭(2) E♭(1) B♭(2) B♭(2) E♭(1)

B Tap this rhythm while counting out loud; repeat until memorized. Then tap the rhythm with your right hand while playing the chord progression with your left. Finally, make up your own rhythms to go with the left hand chord progression.

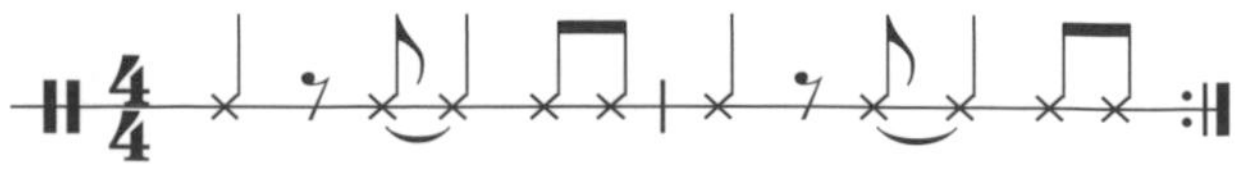

Improv Tools

There are other Improv Tools you can use to "spice up" your improvisation. You can also mix scale and arpeggio-based ideas.

Sequence: play an idea and then repeat it transposed to start on a different note:

Direction Change: play an idea and then send it back the other way:

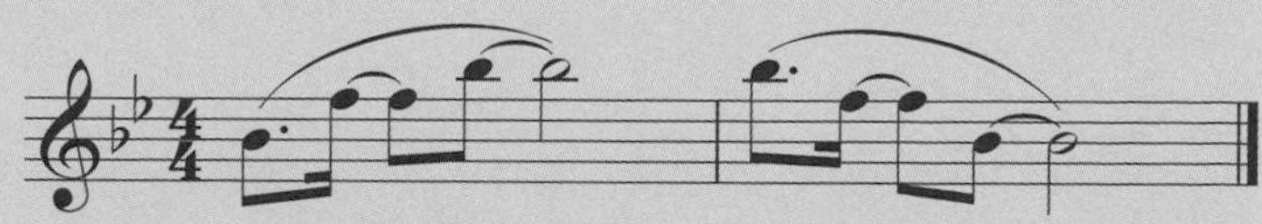

Thirds: use an idea that works in thirds:

C Using the Improv Notes Set as indicated in the score, play various right hand improvisations. Use the Improv Tools, above and in the previous Modules, to get started. Practice *with* the backing track.

Set A
Improv notes:

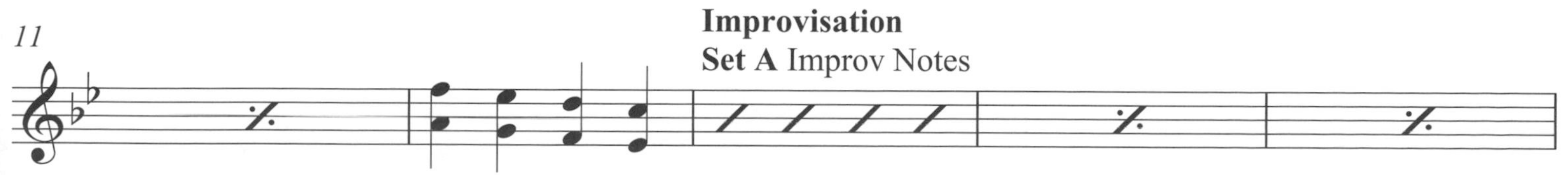

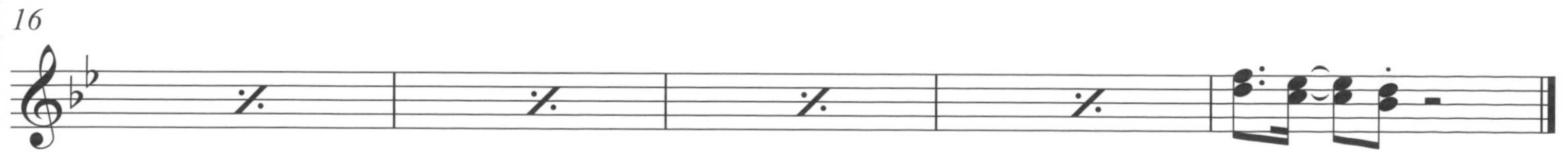

D Now improvise hands together. Practice first *without*, then *with* the backing track.

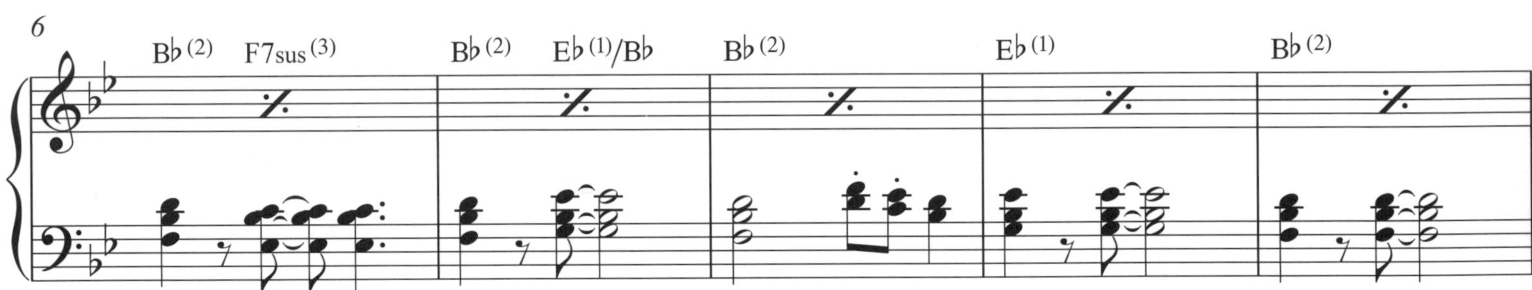

✔ **Improv Tip:** *Try using Grace Notes in only a few places so they don't lose their flair.*

Vamping Tools

Your vamp can use a combination of blocked and broken chords in the right hand. Here are three stimulating options.

Vamp Idea 1:

Idea 2:

Idea 3:

E Vamp various right hand accompaniments using the chords [in brackets] indicated below. Use the Vamping Tools, above and in the previous Modules, to get started. Practice first *without*, then *with* the backing track.

B♭(2) E♭(1)/B♭ B♭(2) F7sus(3) B♭(2) E♭(1)/B♭ B♭(2) B♭(2) E♭(1)/B♭

6 B♭(2) F7sus(3) B♭(2) E♭(1)/B♭ B♭(2) E♭(1) B♭(2)

11 E♭(1) B♭(2) E♭(1)/B♭ B♭(2) F7sus(3) B♭(2) E♭(1)/B♭

16 B♭(2) B♭(2) E♭(1)/B♭ B♭(2) F7sus(3) B♭(2) E♭(1)/B♭

Improv Etude - A Day on the Beach

Module 1

Concept: major 6 chords

A **major 6 chord** (also known as a 6 chord) combines a major triad (e.g., C-E-G) with a major 6th above the root (e.g., A). Sometimes this is done using all four notes (e.g., C-E-G-A) or sometimes it is done using only three notes to achieve the same sound.

6 chords may be written in **first inversion**. In a first inversion 6 chord, the third of the chord is on the bottom. One way to change a root position 6 chord to first inversion is to take the root off the bottom and put it on top.

For improvising on *A Day on the Beach*, all 4 notes will be used in the 6 chords.

A Label the first inversion 6 chords with their lettername (e.g., C6) and a bracketed 1 for "first inversion". Practice the left hand first *without*, then *with* the backing track.

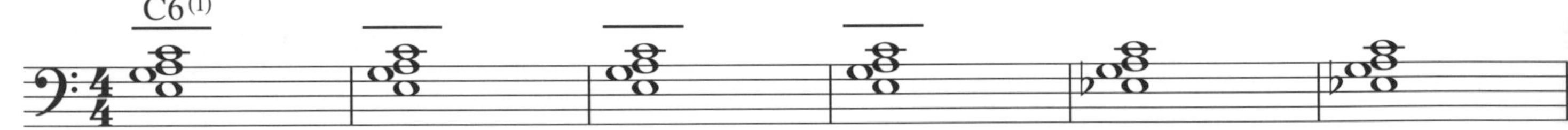

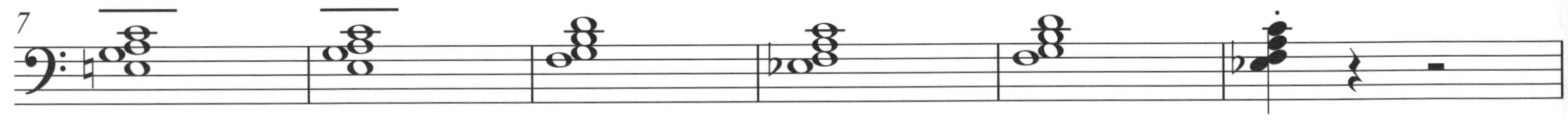

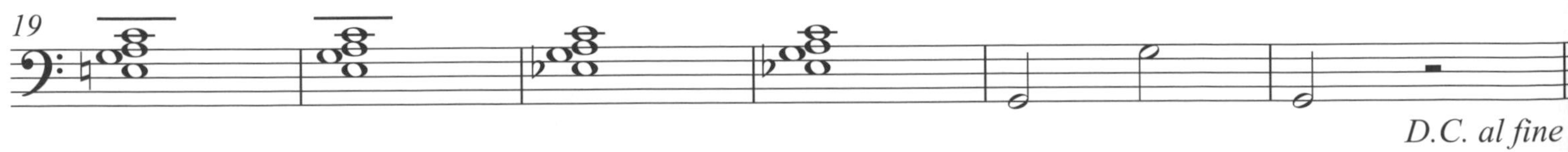

B Tap this rhythm while counting out loud; repeat until memorized. Then tap the rhythm with your right hand while playing the chord progression with your left. Finally, make up your own rhythms to go with the left hand chord progression.

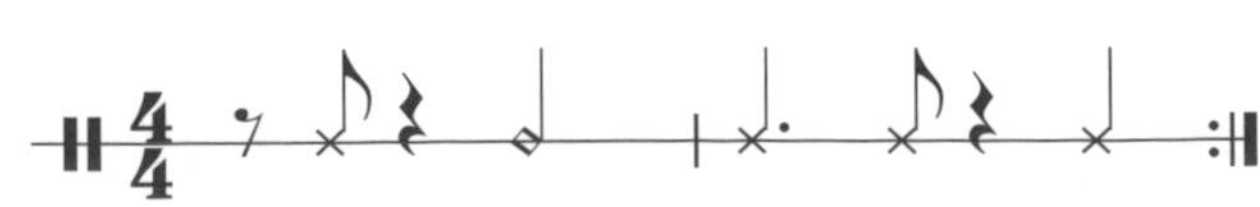

Improv Tools

To improvise on *A Day on the Beach*, you will use two different sets of Improv Notes: one based on the **C major scale**, the other based on the **C melodic minor scale** (ascending).

One way to describe C melodic minor ascending is as a **C major scale** with an E♭ instead of an E♮.

C melodic minor scale

There are specific Improv Tools you can use to make your improvisation interesting and musical.

Rhythmic Shift: play a scale-based idea and then restate it starting on a different beat in the bar:

Call & Response: play an idea and then "answer" it with a contrasting idea:

C Using the Improv Notes Set A or B as indicated in the score, play various right hand improvisations. Use the Improv Tools, above, to get started. Practice *with* the backing track.

13 **Improvisation**
Set B Improv Notes

FINE

Improvisation
Set A Improv Notes

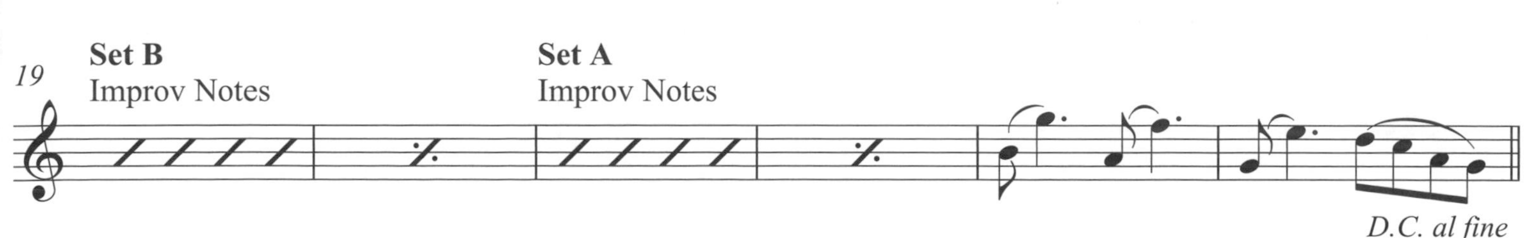

D Now improvise hands together. Practice first *without*, then *with* the backing track.

✔ **Improv Tip:** *When you're playing scale-based melodies, using fewer notes can be very effective.*

Vamping Tools

Vamping is an improvised accompaniment style often featuring chords in the right hand against single notes in the left hand. When vamping with blocked chords in the right hand, you can use various rhythmic patterns and syncopations to create interest.

Vamp Idea 1:

Idea 2 – reversing the order of rhythmic pattern 1:

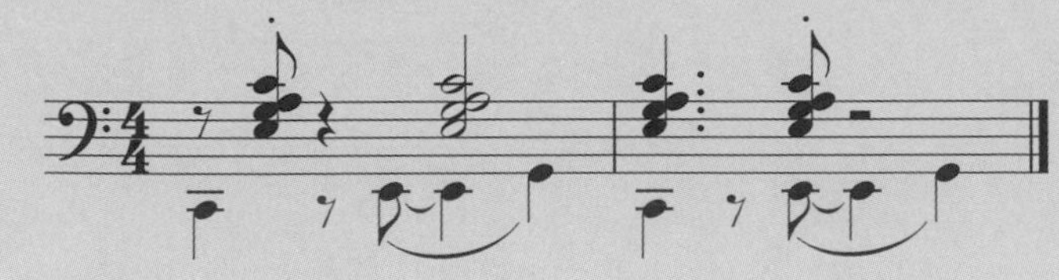

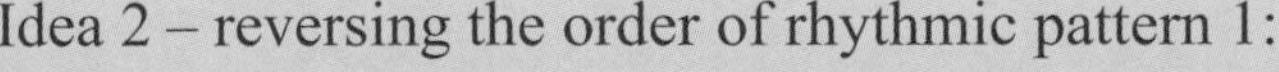

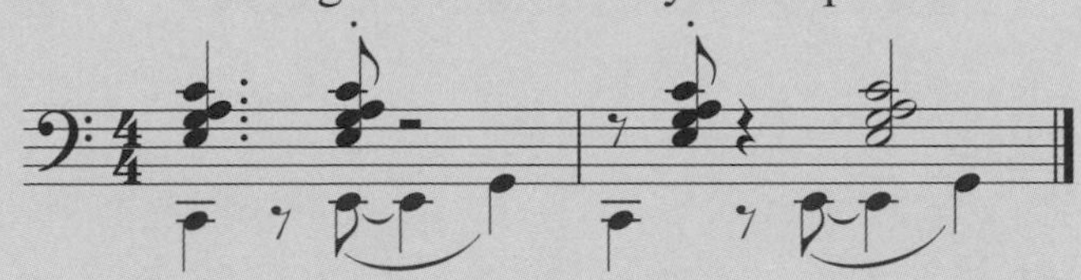

Idea 3 – adding syncopated chords to each bar:

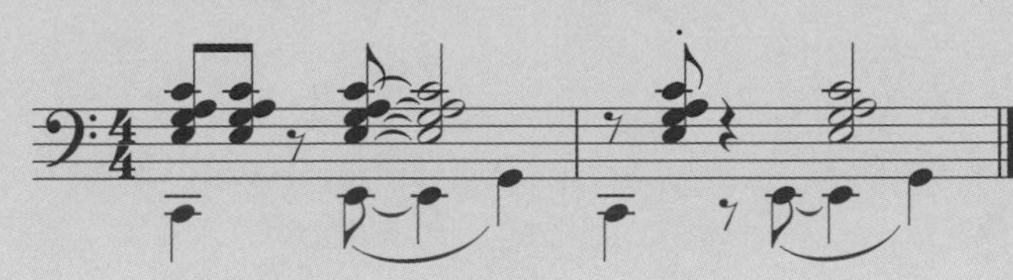

E Vamp various right hand accompaniments using the chords [in brackets] indicated below. Use the Vamping Tools, above, to get started. Practice first *without*, then *with* the backing track.

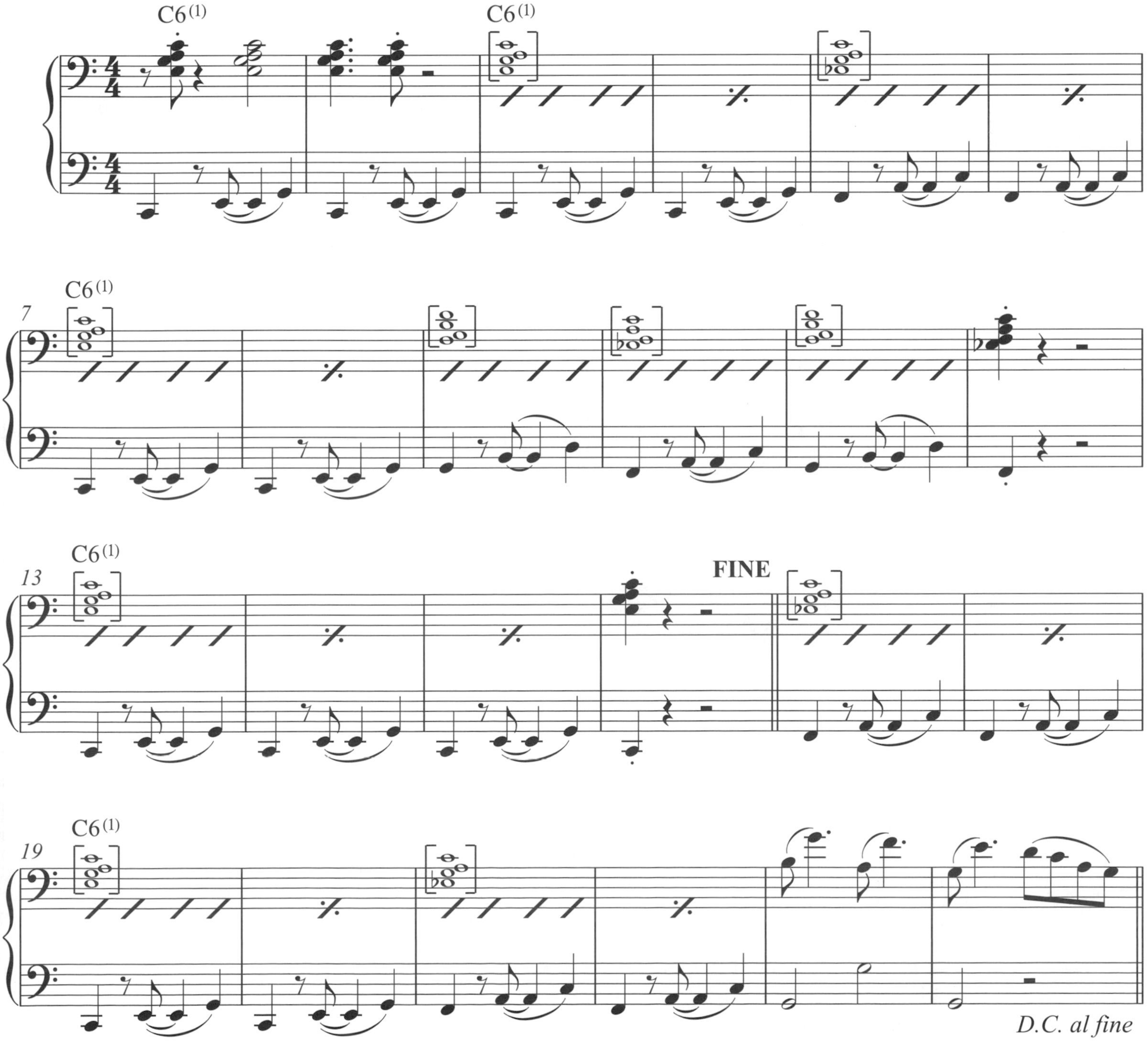

C6(1)
C6(1)
7
C6(1)
13
C6(1)
FINE
19
C6(1)
D.C. al fine

Improv Etude - A Day on the Beach

Module 2

Concept: Dominant 7 chords

A **Dominant 7 chord** (also known as a 7 chord) combines a major triad (e.g., G-E-D) with a minor 7th above the root (e.g., F). Sometimes this is done using all four notes (e.g., G-E-D-F), but often it is done with only three notes to achieve the same sound.

7 chords may be written in **third inversion**. In a third inversion 7 chord, the minor seventh of the chord is on the bottom. One way to change a root position 7 chord to third inversion is to take the 7th off the top and put it on bottom.

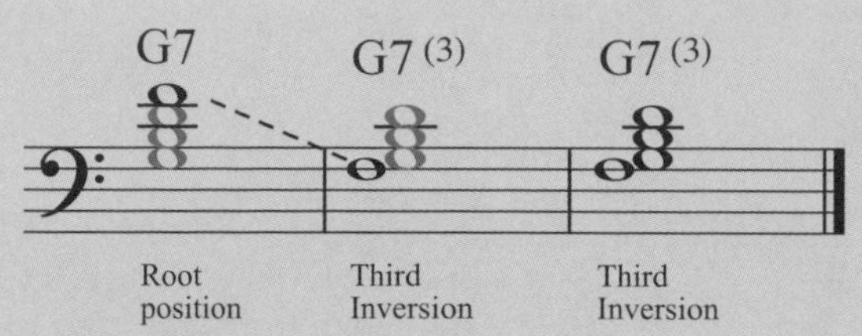

For improvising on *A Day on the Beach*, all 4 notes will be used in the 7 chords.

A Label the third inversion 7 chords with their lettername (e.g., G7 or F7) and a bracketed 3 for "third inversion". Practice the left hand first *without*, then *with* the backing track.

B Tap this rhythm while counting out loud; repeat until memorized. Then tap the rhythm with your right hand while playing the chord progression with your left. Finally, make up your own rhythms to go with the left hand chord progression.

Improv Tools

Idea & Variation is another Improv Tool you can use, in addition to **Rhythmic Shift** and **Call & Response**.

Your improvisation can also use arpeggio-based ideas.

Rhythmic Shift: play an arpeggio-based idea, then restate it starting on a different beat in the bar:

Call & Response: play an idea and then "answer" it with a contrasting idea:

Idea & Variation: play an arpeggio-based idea and then repeat it with a slight variation:

C Using the Improv Notes Set A or B as indicated in the score, play various right hand improvisations. Use the Improv Tools, above and in the previous Module, to get started. Practice *with* the backing track.

Set A
Improv notes:

Set B
Improv notes:

Improvisation
Set A Improv Notes

7 **Set B**
Improv Notes

13 **Improvisation**
Set B Improv Notes

FINE **Improvisation**
Set A Improv Notes

19 **Set B**
Improv Notes

Set A
Improv Notes

D.C. al fine

D Now improvise hands together. Practice first *without*, then *with* the backing track.

✔ **Improv Tip:** *The left hand is also an important part of your improvisation. Try varying it rhythmically by spontaneously adding accents to complement what you're doing with your right hand.*

Vamping Tools

Here are three more vamping ideas for *A Day on the Beach*, this time using a combination of blocked and broken chords.

Vamp Idea 1 – blocked chords on the off-beats:

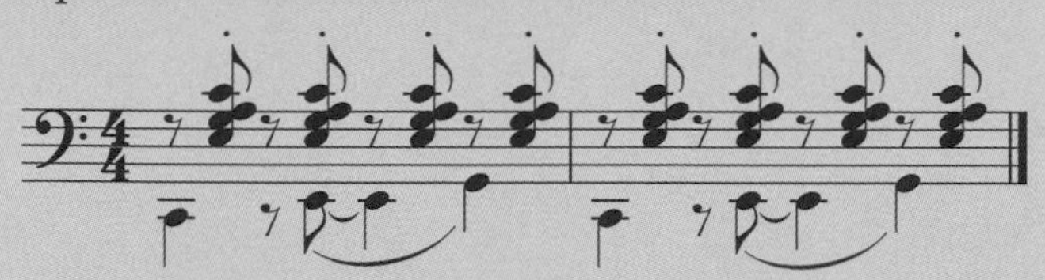

Idea 2 – a combination of broken and blocked chords:

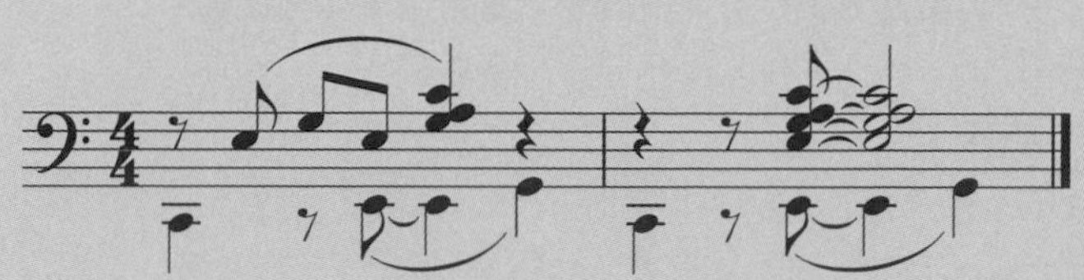

Idea 3 – a 3+3+2 pattern in the right hand:

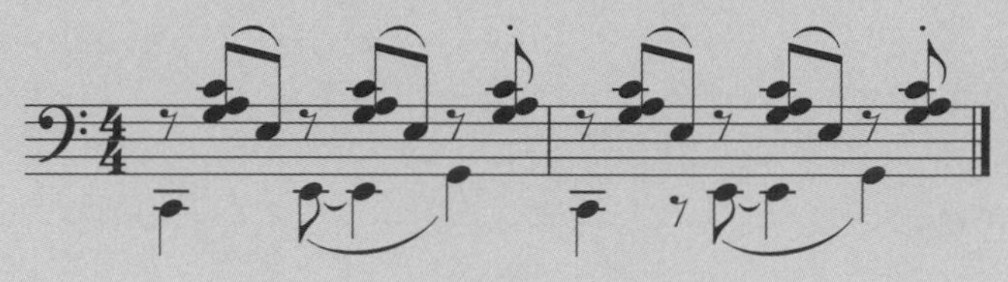

E Vamp various right hand accompaniments using the chords [in brackets] indicated below. Use the Vamping Tools, above and in the previous Module, to get started. Practice first *without*, then *with* the backing track.

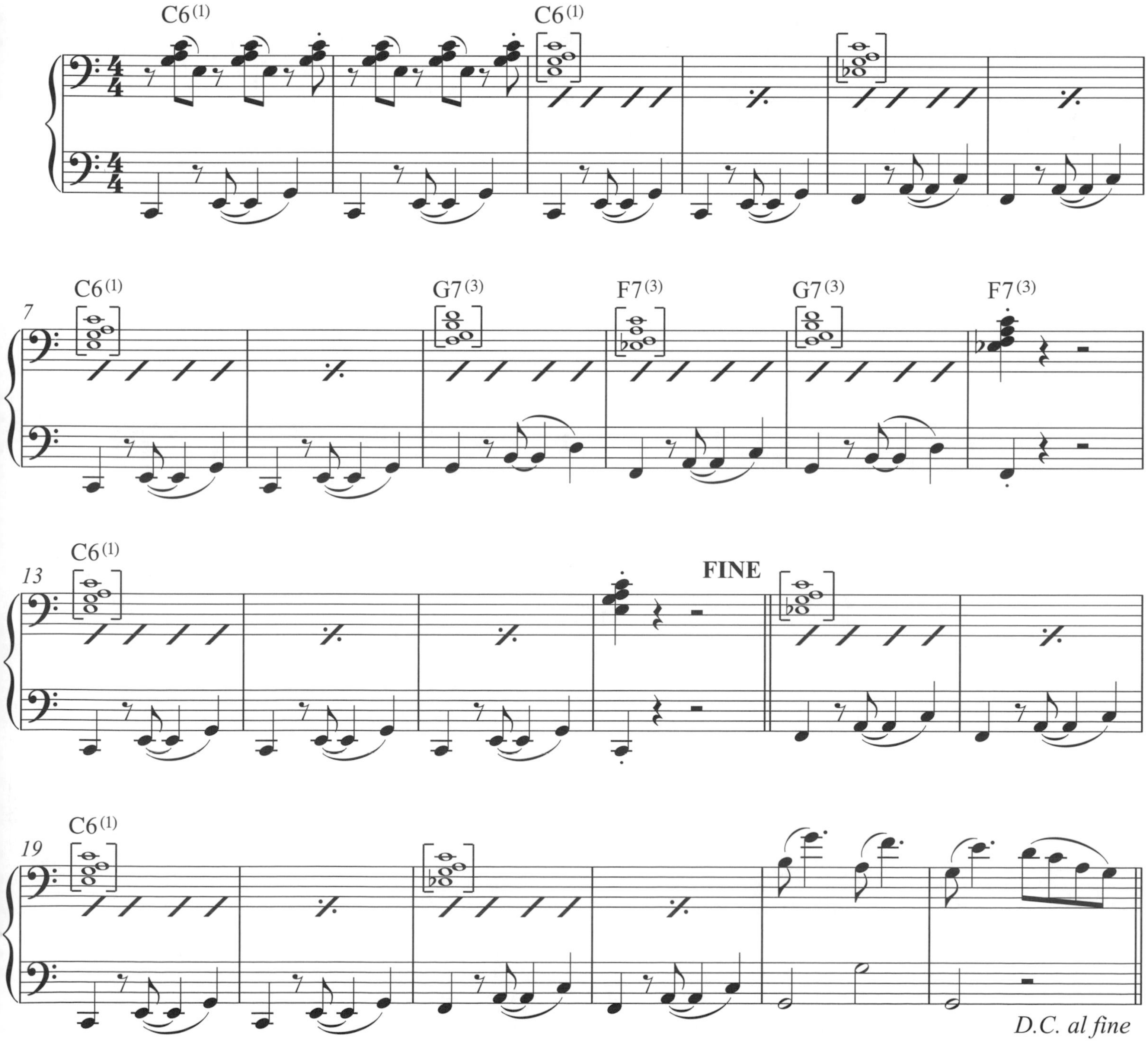
C6(1)
C6(1)
7
C6(1)
G7(3)
F7(3)
G7(3)
F7(3)
13
C6(1)
FINE
19
C6(1)
D.C. al fine

Improv Etude - A Day on the Beach

Module 3

Concept: 9 chords

A **9 chord** is a **7 chord** with the 9th scale degree added. Sometimes this is done using all five notes – a major triad (e.g., F-A-C) with the minor 7th (e.g., E♭) and major 9th (e.g., G) added (e.g., F-A-C-E♭-G) – or sometimes it is done with only four notes to achieve the same sound.

9 chords may be written in **third inversion**. In a third inversion 9 chord, the seventh of the chord is on the bottom.

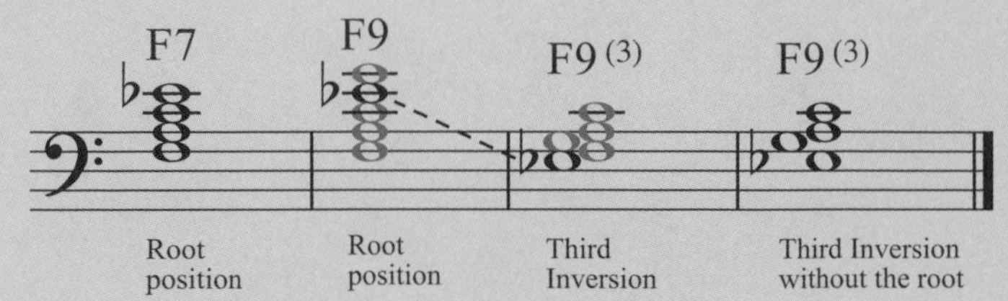

One way to change a root position 9 chord to third inversion is to take the 7th off from near the top – just underneath the 9th – and put it on the bottom.

For improvising on *A Day on the Beach*, the root will be left out.

A Label the third inversion 9 chords with their lettername (e.g., F9) and a bracketed 3 for "third inversion". Practice the left hand first *without*, then *with* the backing track.

C6 (1) F9 (3)

7 C6 (1) G7 (3) F7 (3) G7 (3) F7 (3)

13 C6 (1) FINE

19 C6 (1)

D.C. al fine

B Tap this rhythm while counting out loud; repeat until memorized. Then tap the rhythm with your right hand while playing the chord progression with your left. Finally, make up your own rhythms to go with the left hand chord progression.

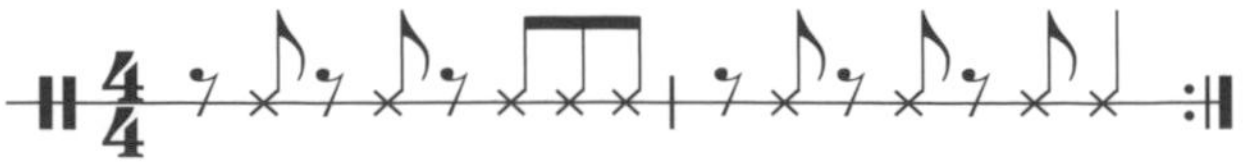

Improv Tools

There are other Improv Tools you can use to add color and interest to your improvisation. These Tools can be used with either scale-based or arpeggio-based ideas.

Grace Notes: a great way to "spice up" your improvisation:

Direction Change: play a scale-based idea that changes direction to create contrast:

Thirds: play your musical idea in thirds to add further expressiveness to a melody:

C Using the Improv Notes Set A or B as indicated in the score, play various right hand improvisations. Use the Improv Tools, above and in the previous Modules, to get started. Practice *with* the backing track.

Set A
Improv notes:

Set B
Improv notes:

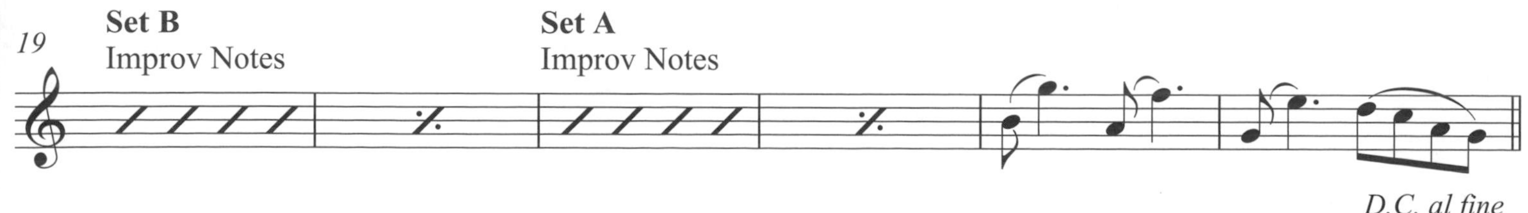

D Now improvise hands together. Practice first *without*, then *with* the backing track.

✔ **Improv Tip:** *Grace Notes won't sound right on every note of your improvisation. Experiment to find the ones which sound best to you.*

Vamping Tools

Here are three more vamping ideas for *A Day on the Beach* which combine blocked and broken chords.

Vamp Idea 1:

Idea 2:

Idea 3:

E Vamp various right hand accompaniments using the chords [in brackets] indicated below. Use the Vamping Tools, above and in the previous Modules, to get started. Practice first *without*, then *with* the backing track.

C6 (1) C6 (1) F9 (3)

7 C6 (1) G7 (3) F7 (3) G7 (3) F7 (3)

13 C6 (1) FINE F9 (3)

19 C6 (1) F9 (3)

D.C. al fine

Improv Etude - Big Blue

Module 1

Concept: Dominant 7 and 9 chords

A **Dominant 7** (or **7 chord**) combines a major triad (e.g., G-B-D) with a minor 7th above the root (e.g., F♮). A **9 chord** is a 7 chord with the addition of the 9th above the root (e.g., C-E-G-B♭-D).

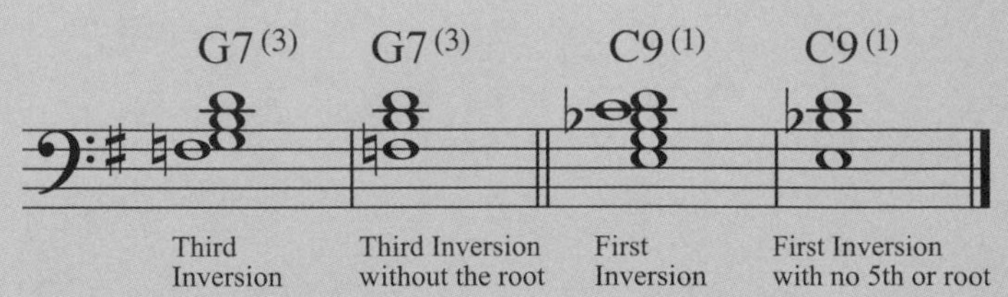

7 and 9 chords may be written in **first** and **third inversion**. In a first inversion chord, the third of the chord is on the bottom. In a third inversion chord, the minor seventh of the chord is on the bottom. To review changing root position chords to first or third inversion, see Modules 1 & 2 of *Barbican Blues* (pp. 2 & 6). For improvising on *Big Blue*, the root of the 7(3) and root and 5th of the 9(1) chords will be left out.

A Label the first inversion 9 and third inversion 7 chords with their lettername (e.g., G7 or C9) and a bracketed "1" or "3" for the inversion. Practice the left hand first *without*, then *with* the backing track.

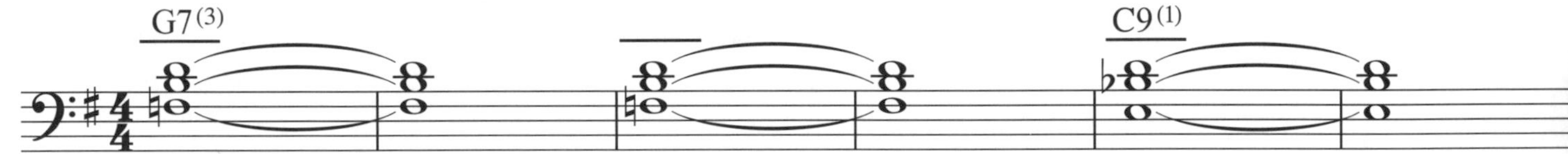

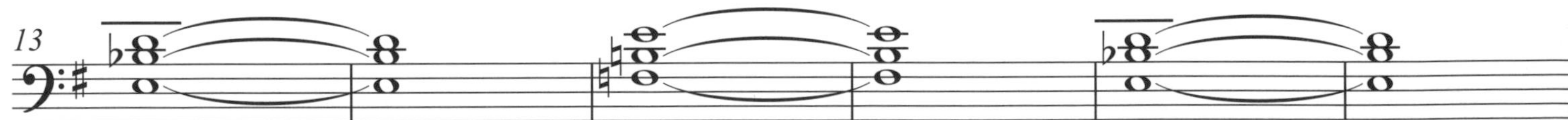

D.C. al coda

B Tap this rhythm while counting out loud; repeat until memorized. Then tap the rhythm with your right hand while playing the chord progression with your left. Finally, make up your own rhythms to go with the left hand chord progression.

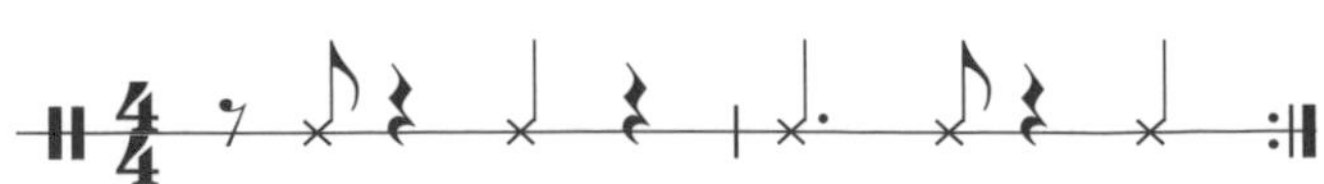

Improv Tools

To improvise on *Big Blue*, you will use the **G Blues scale**.

One way to describe the G Blues scale is as a G **minor pentatonic** (G, B♭, C, D, F♮) with an added lowered 5th scale degree (D♭).

G blues scale

There are specific Improv Tools you can use to make your improvisation interesting and musical.

Rhythmic Shift: play an idea and then re-state it starting on a different beat in the bar:

Pedal Notes: a pedal note is a repeated note that doesn't change when the melody moves. Here the G's are pedal notes "above":

C Using the Improv Notes Set as indicated in the score, play various right hand improvisations. Use the Improv Tools, above, to get started. Practice *with* the backing track.

Set A
Improv notes:

D Now improvise hands together. Practice first *without*, then *with* the backing track.

✔ **Improv Tip:** *Try using one of the Improv Tools through your whole improvisation.*

Vamping Tools

Vamping is an improvised accompaniment, often with chords in the right hand against single notes in the left. You can vary blocked right hand chords by changing the pattern of the rhythms.

Right hand rhythmic pattern 1:

Pattern 2:

Pattern 3:

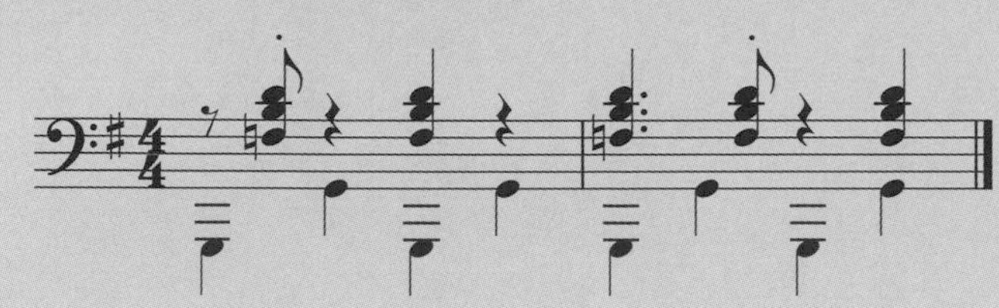

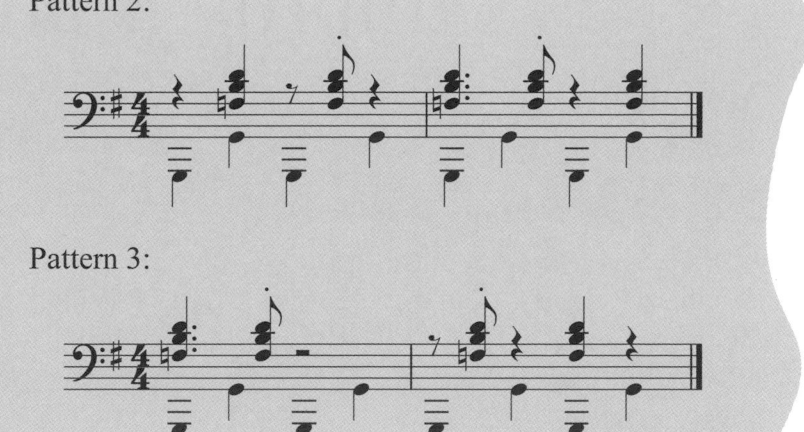

E Vamp various right hand accompaniments using the chords [in brackets] indicated below. Use the Vamping Tools, above, to get started. Practice first *without*, then *with* the backing track.

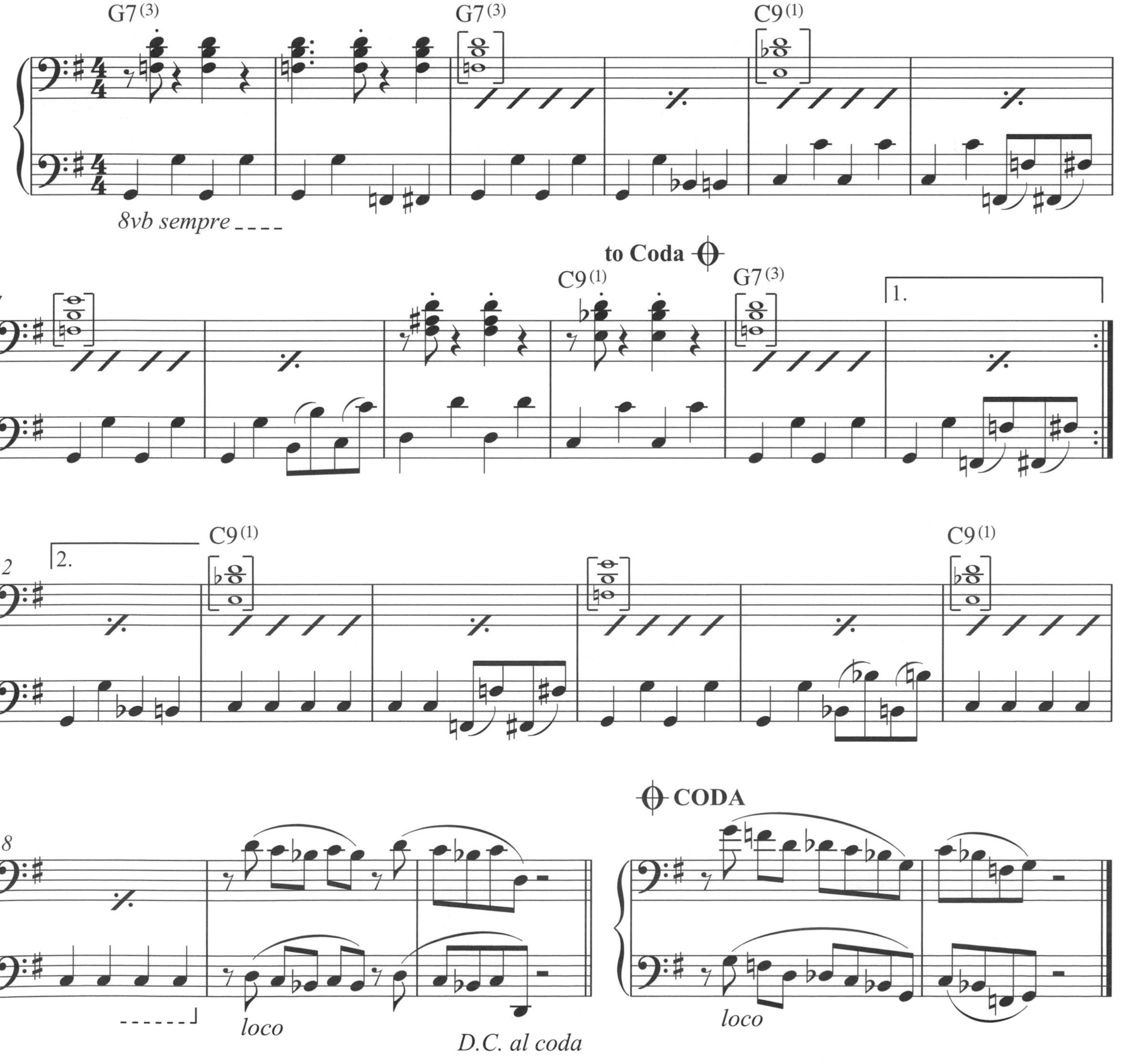
G7(3)
G7(3)
C9(1)
8vb sempre
to Coda
C9(1)
G7(3)
1.
2.
C9(1)
C9(1)
CODA
loco
D.C. al coda
loco

Improv Etude - Big Blue

Module 2

Concept: Dominant 13 chords

Like the **9 chord**, a **13 chord** (e.g., G13) extends a dominant 7 chord by adding a 9th, 11th, and 13th to the chord (e.g., G-B-D-F♮-A-C-E). Sometimes the 9th and often the 11th are left out, but the foundation 7 chord is always present.

13 chords may be written in **third inversion**. In a third inversion 13 chord, the seventh degree of the scale is on the bottom. To review changing root position chords to third inversion, see Module 2 of *Barbican Blues* (pg. 6).

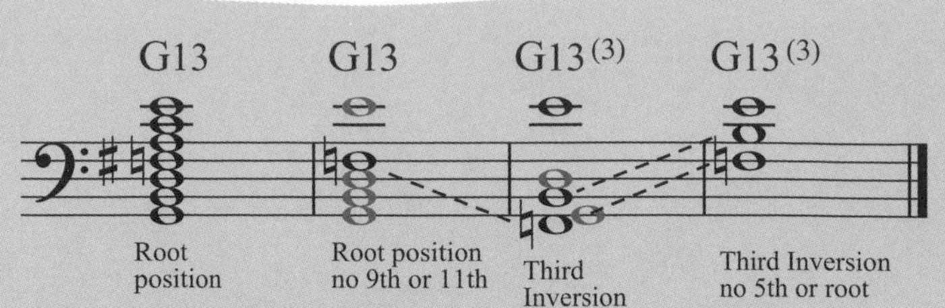

In the *Big Blue* improvisation, the root, 5th, 9th, and 11th will be left out. The "G" root note is played in the backing track, achieving the G13 sound when combined with the left hand chord.

A Label the third inversion 13 chords with their lettername (e.g., G13) and a bracketed 3 for "third inversion". Practice the left hand first *without*, then *with* the backing track.

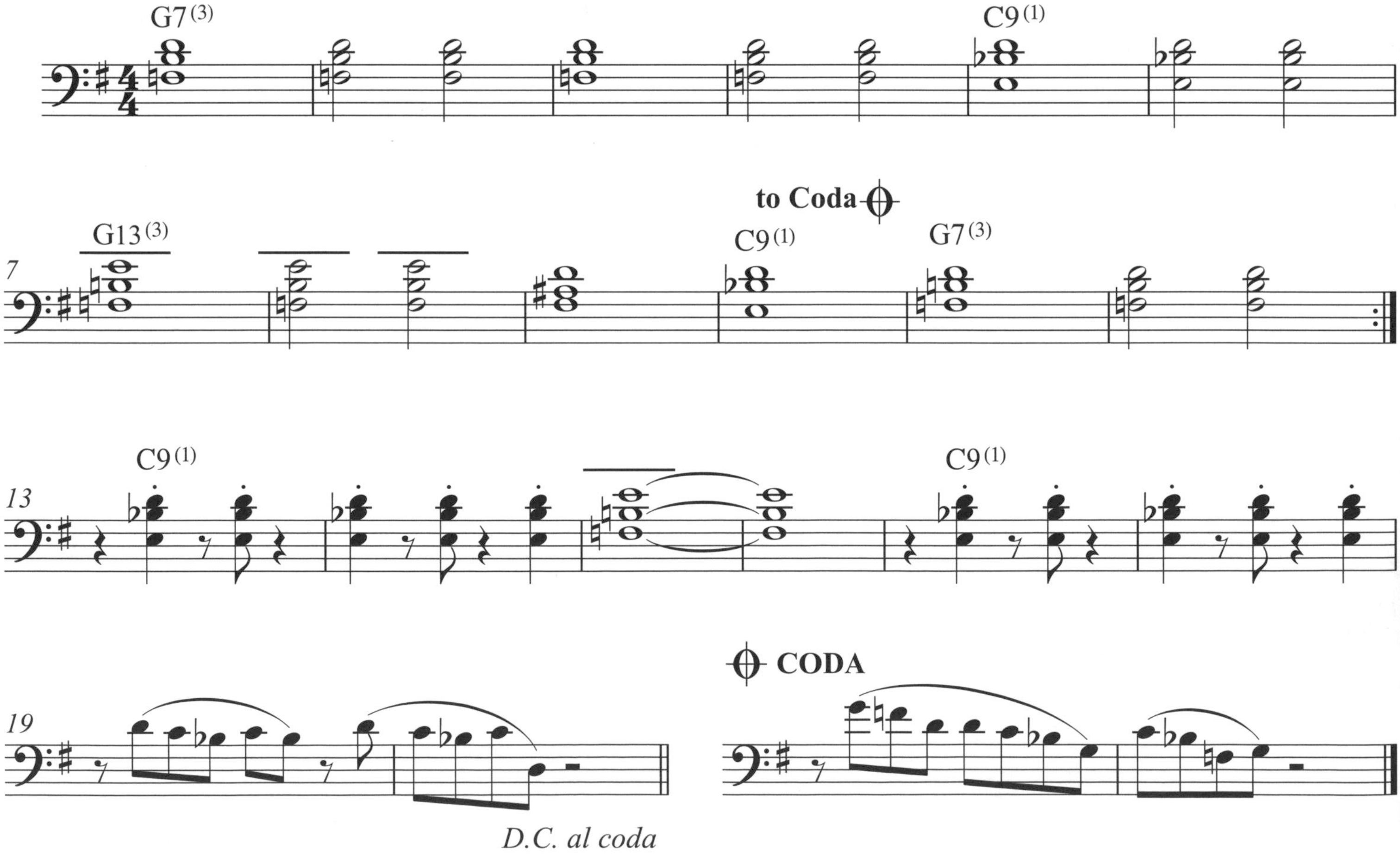

G7 (3) C9 (1)

7 G13 (3) **to Coda** C9 (1) G7 (3)

13 C9 (1) C9 (1)

19

D.C. al coda

CODA

B Tap this rhythm while counting out loud; repeat until memorized. Then tap the rhythm with your right hand while playing the chord progression with your left. Finally, make up your own rhythms to go with the left hand chord progression.

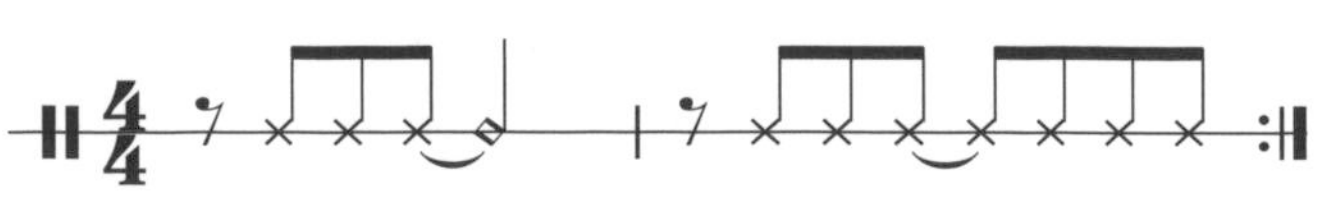

Improv Tools

Improvisations can also use **Chording**, chords in both hands, to create a full, rich effect, in addition to **Rhythmic Shift** and **Pedal Notes**.

Rhythmic Shift: play an idea and then re-state it starting on a different beat:

Pedal Notes: a pedal note is a repeated note that doesn't change when the melody moves. Here the G's are pedal notes "above":

Chording: play chords in both hands to create contrast and rich harmonic effects:

C Using the Improv Notes Set as indicated in the score, play various right hand improvisations. Use the Improv Tools, above and in the previous Module, to get started. Practice *with* the backing track.

Set A
Improv notes:

D Now improvise hands together. Practice first *without*, then *with* the backing track.

✔ **Improv Tip:** *When you use Call & Response, imagine two different instruments answering each other, for example trumpet and sax.*

Vamping Tools

Vamps can also use broken chords in the right hand. You can create interest by varying the starting note of the arpeggio.

Vamp Idea 1 – start from the bottom note of the chord:

Idea 2: start from the top note of the chord:

Idea 3: start from the middle note of the chord:

E Vamp various accompaniments using the chords [in brackets] indicated below. Use the Vamping Tools, above and in the previous Module, to get started. Practice first *without*, then *with* the backing track.

G7(3) G7(3) C9(1)

8vb sempre

7 G13(3) C9(1) **to Coda** G7(3) 1.

12 2. C9(1) G13(3) C9(1)

18 **CODA**

loco *D.C. al coda* *loco*

Improv Etude - Big Blue

Module 3

Concept: augmented chords

An **augmented chord** (**aug**) is a major chord with a raised 5th instead of a perfect 5th (e.g., D-F♯-A♯).

Augmented chords may be written in **first inversion**. In a first inversion aug chord, the third degree of the scale is on the bottom. Aug chords are changed from root position to first inversion the same way as other chords.

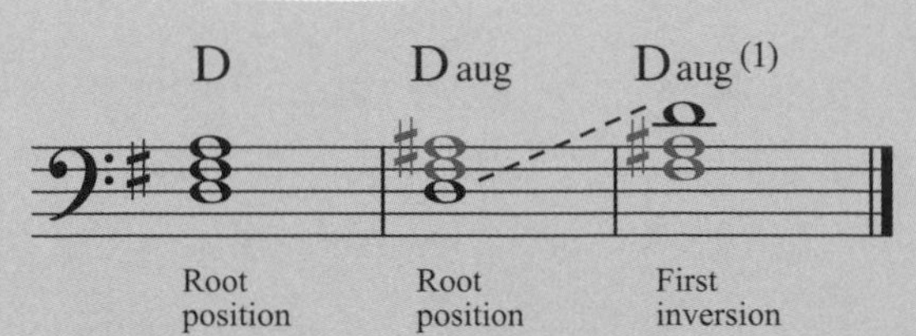

To review changing root position chords to first inversion, see Module 1 of *Barbican Blues* (pg. 2) and Module 2 of *Sparkling* (pg. 18).

A Label the chord progression with the lettername, (e.g., G7, C9, G13, or Daug) and a bracketed number "1" or "3" for the correct inversion. It is common when labelling a chord progression to identify chords only when they are different from the previous chord. Practice the left hand first *without*, then *with* the backing track.

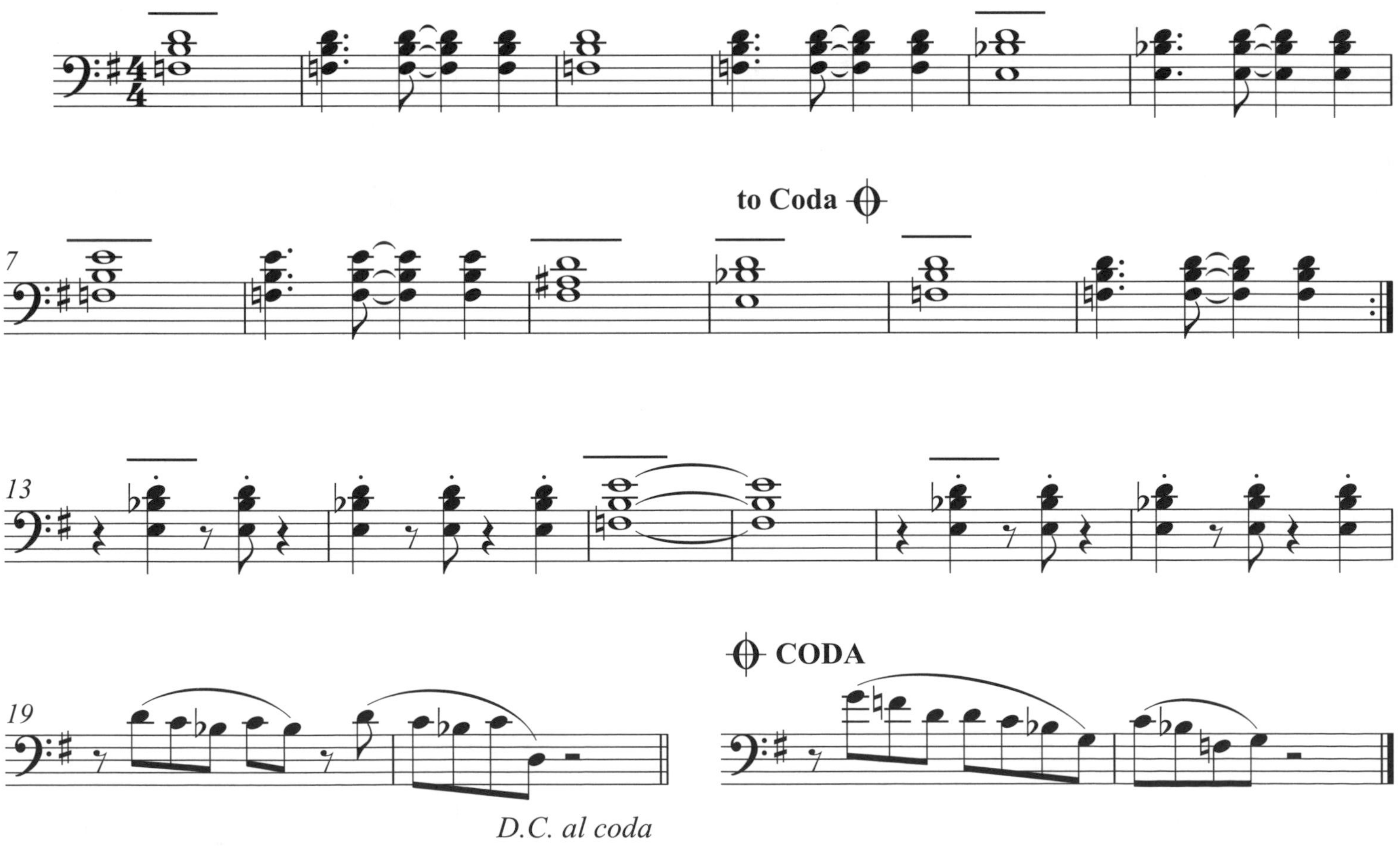

7 — to Coda

13

19 — *D.C. al coda*

CODA

B Tap this rhythm while counting out loud; repeat until memorized. Then tap the rhythm with your right hand while playing the chord progression with your left. Finally, make up your own rhythms to go with the left hand chord progression.

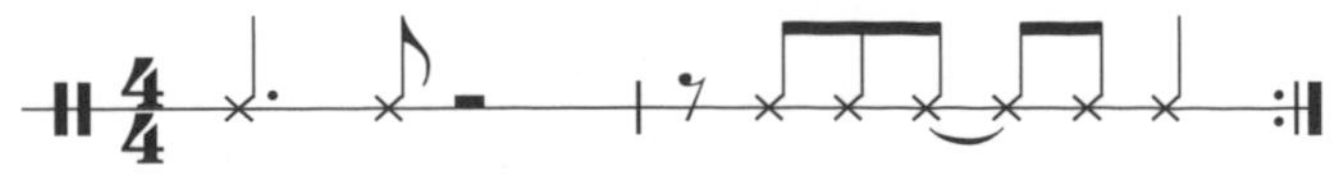

Improv Tools

There are other Improv Tools you can use to make your improvisation ideas more interesting and musical.

Grace Notes: add extra "bite" to your improvisation with grace notes:

Continuous Run: play a running stream of continuous eighth notes:

Idea & Variation: create an idea and then repeat it slightly varied:

C Using the Improv Notes Set as indicated in the score, play various right hand improvisations. Use the Improv Tools, above and in the previous Modules, to get started. Practice *with* the backing track.

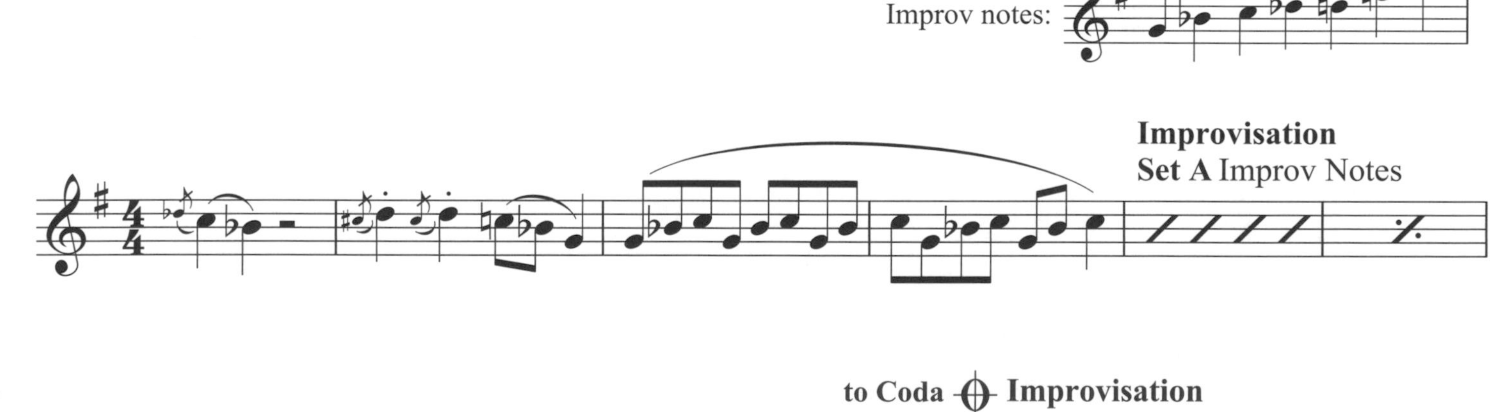

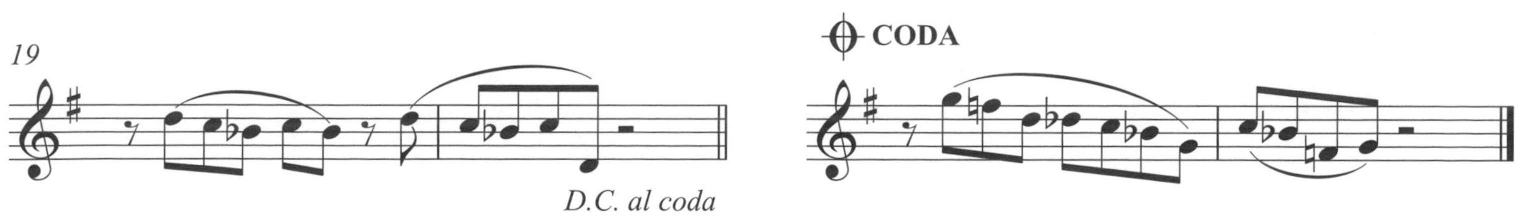

D Now improvise hands together. Practice first *without*, then *with* the backing track.

Improv Tip: *See how long you can keep a continuous stream of eighth notes going in your improvisation!*

Vamping Tools

There are all kinds of patterns you can create in your vamp using blocked or broken chords, or a combination of the two.

Vamp Idea 1 – blocked chords followed by arpeggios:

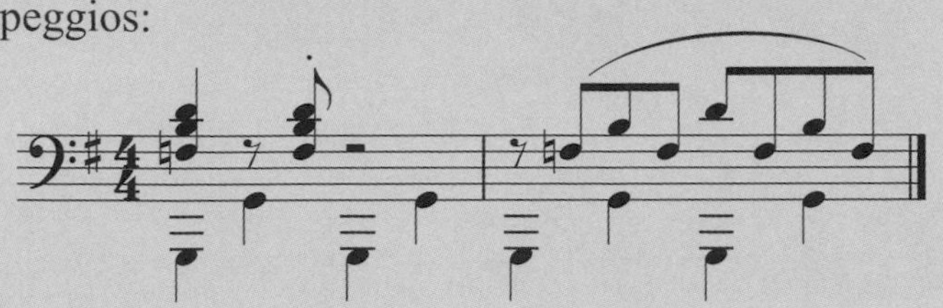

Idea 2: blocked chords only:

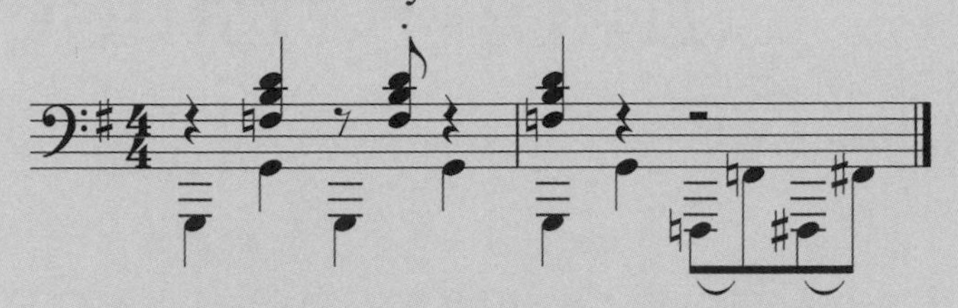

Idea 3: arpeggios followed by blocked chords:

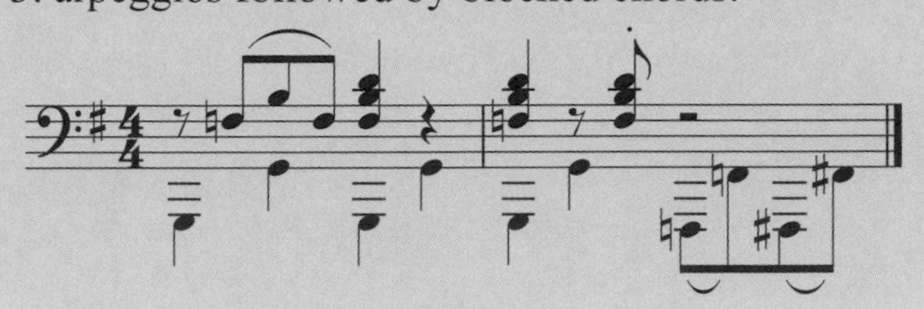

E Vamp various accompaniments using the chords [in brackets] indicated below. Use the Vamping Tools, above and in the previous Modules, to get started. Practice first *without*, then *with* the backing track.

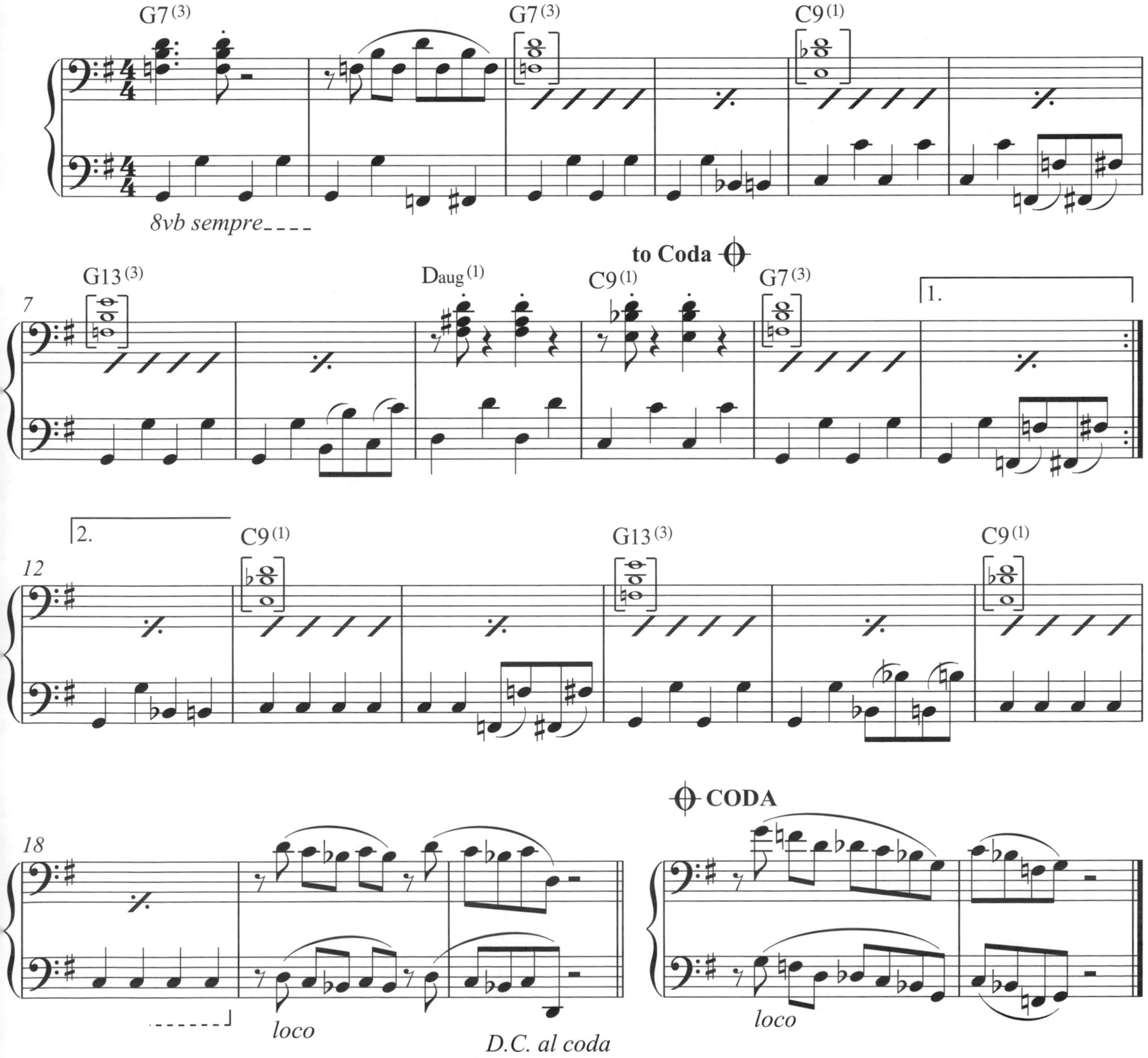

G7(3)
G7(3)
C9(1)
8vb sempre
to Coda
7
G13(3)
Daug(1)
C9(1)
G7(3)
1.
2.
12
C9(1)
G13(3)
C9(1)
CODA
18
loco
D.C. al coda
loco

Improv Etude - Up and About

Module 1

Concept: major 7 & major 9 chords

A **major 7 chord (maj7)** combines a major triad (e.g., F-A-C) with a major 7th above the root (e.g., E). This is the same construction as the 7 chord, only using a major 7th instead of minor 7th. Similarly, a **major 9 chord (maj9)** adds a 9th above the root to the maj7 chord (e.g., F-A-C-E-G).

Major 9 chords may be written in **fourth inversion**. In a fourth inversion chord, the ninth of the chord is on the bottom. One way to change a root position maj9 chord to fourth inversion is to take the 9th off the top and put it on the bottom; you'll also lose the root or move it up an octave. To review third inversion, see Module 2 of *Barbican Blues* (pg. 6).

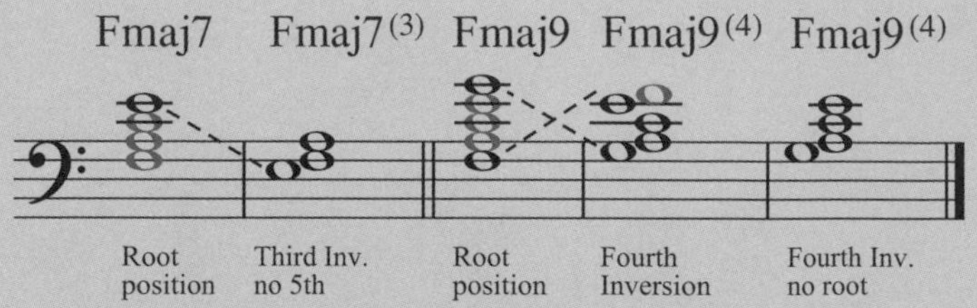

In the *Up and About* improvisation, the root of the maj9(4) chords is played in the backing track.

A Label the maj7 and maj9 chords with their lettername (e.g., Fmaj7, Fmaj9, or E♭maj9) and a bracketed "3" or "4" for the correct inversion. Practice the left hand first *without*, then *with* the backing track.

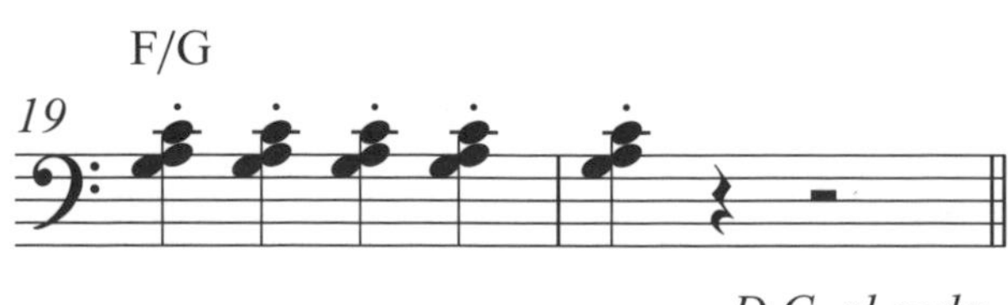

D.C. al coda
(no repeat)

B Tap this rhythm while counting out loud; repeat until memorized. Then tap the rhythm with your right hand while playing the chord progression with your left. Finally, make up your own rhythms to go with the left hand chord progression.

Improv Tools

To improvise on *Up and About*, you will use two sets of Improv Notes: one based on the **G Mixolydian mode**, the other based on the **G Dorian mode**.

One way to describe G Mixolydian is as a G Major scale with an F♮ instead of an F♯. One way to describe G Dorian is as a G natural minor scale with an E♮ instead of an E♭.

There are Improv Tools you can use to make your improvisation interesting and musical.

Sequence: play an idea and then repeat it transposed to start on a different note:

Call & Response: play an idea, then "answer" it with a contrasting idea:

C Using the Improv Notes Set A or B as indicated in the score, play various right hand improvisations. Use the Improv Tools, above, to get started. Practice *with* the backing track.

Set A
Improv notes:

Set B
Improv notes:

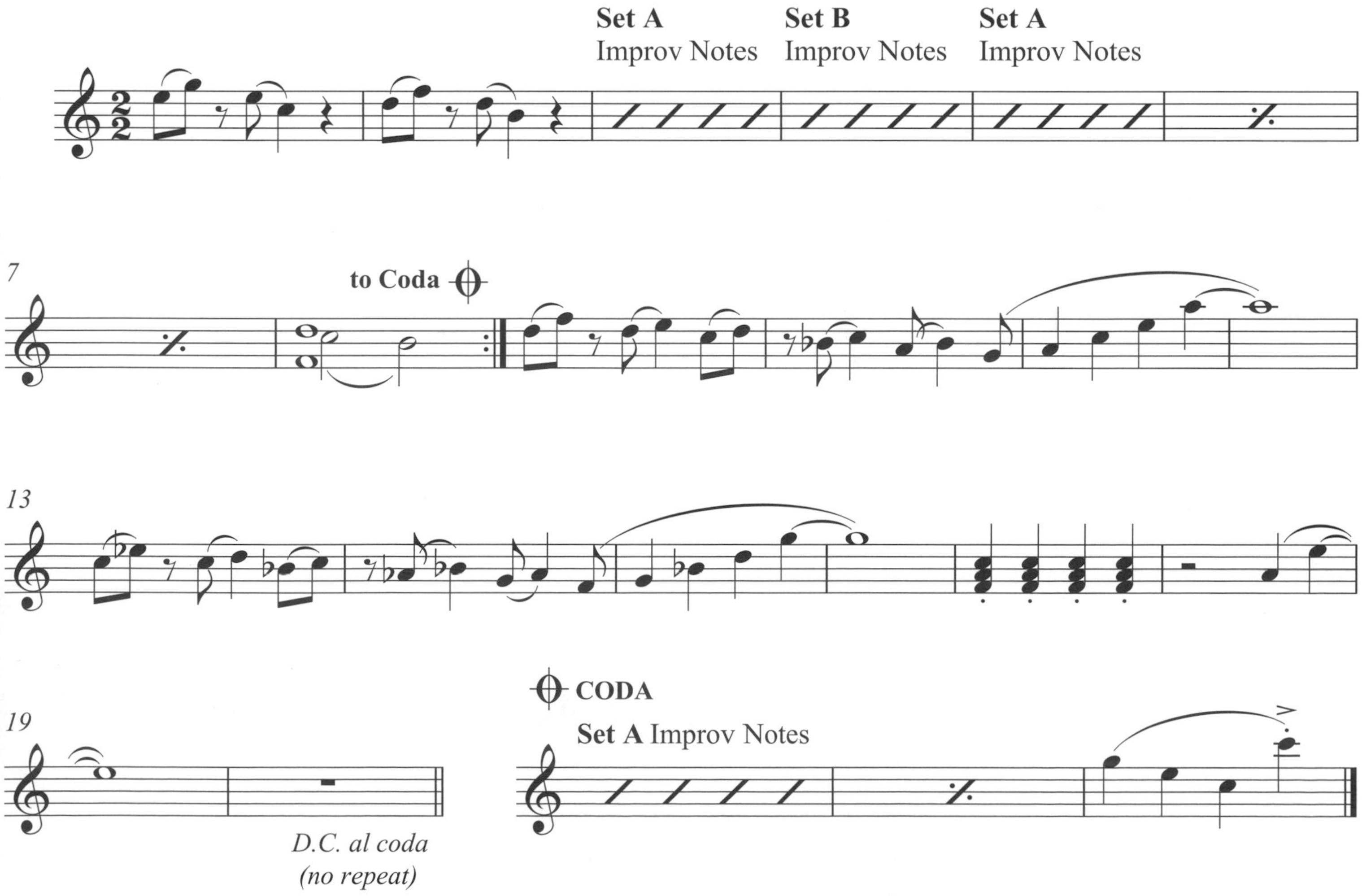

Set A Improv Notes | **Set B** Improv Notes | **Set A** Improv Notes

7

to Coda

13

19

D.C. al coda
(no repeat)

CODA

Set A Improv Notes

D Now improvise hands together. Practice first *without*, then *with* the backing track.

✔ **Improv Tip:** *In very fast pieces, like* Up and About, *keep your improvisation ideas short.*

Vamping Tools

Vamping is an improvised accompaniment, often with chords in the right hand against single notes in the left. In very fast pieces, such as *Up and About*, the right hand chords can focus on rhythmic ideas.

Right hand rhythmic pattern 1:

Right hand rhythmic pattern 2:

Right hand rhythmic pattern 3:

E Vamp various right hand accompaniments using the chords [in brackets] indicated below. Use the Vamping Tools, above, to get started. Practice first *without*, then *with* the backing track.

C (2) Am (2) Fmaj7 (3) E7 (3)

7 Am (2) **to Coda** Fmaj9 (4)

13 E♭maj9 (4)

19 F/G

D.C. al coda (no repeat)

CODA

8

Improv Etude - Up and About

Module 2

Concept: minor 7 & minor 9 chords

A **minor 7 chord (m7)** combines a minor triad (e.g., G-B♭-D) with a minor 7th above the root (e.g., F). This is the same construction as the 7 chord, only based on a minor triad. A **minor 9 chord (m9)** adds a major 9th (e.g., A) above the root to the m7 chord.

Minor 9 chords may be written in **fourth inversion**. In a fourth inversion chord, the ninth of the chord is on the bottom. One way to change a root postion m9 chord to fourth inversion is to take the 9th off the top and put it

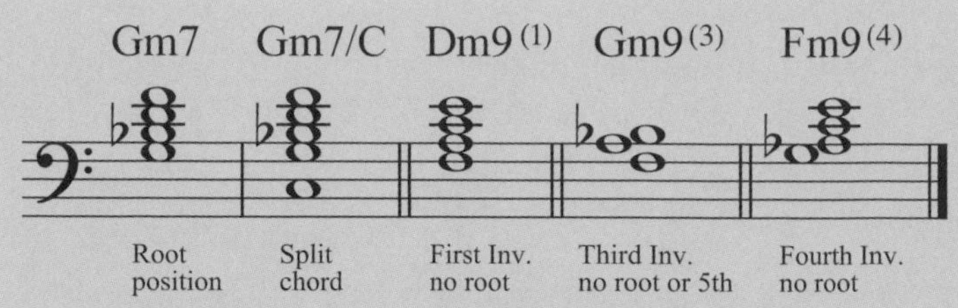

on the bottom; you'll also lose the root or move it up an octave. To review first and third inversion, see Module 3 of *Barbican Blues* (pg. 10) and *A Day on the Beach* (pg. 34).

In the *Up and About* improvisation, the root of the m9 chords is played in the backing track.

A Label the m7 and m9 chords with their lettername (e.g., Gm7, Gm9, Fm9, or Dm9) and a bracketed "1", "3", or"4" for the inversion, as appropriate. Practice the left hand first *without*, then *with* the backing track.

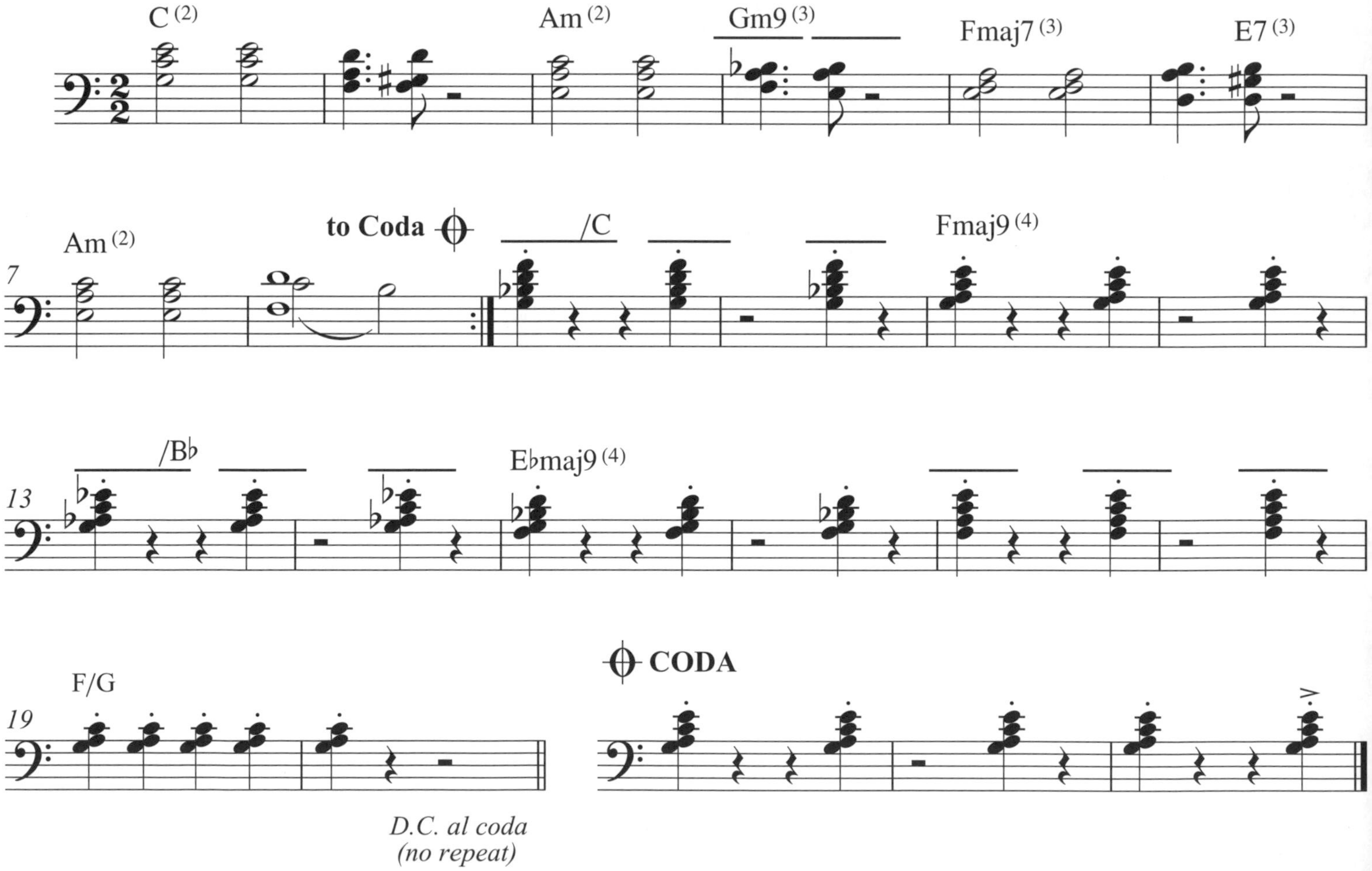

C (2) Am (2) Gm9 (3) Fmaj7 (3) E7 (3)

Am (2) **to Coda** /C Fmaj9 (4)

/B♭ E♭maj9 (4)

F/G

CODA

D.C. al coda (no repeat)

B Tap this rhythm while counting out loud; repeat until memorized. Then tap the rhythm with your right hand while playing the chord progression with your left. Finally, make up your own rhythms to go with the left hand chord progression.

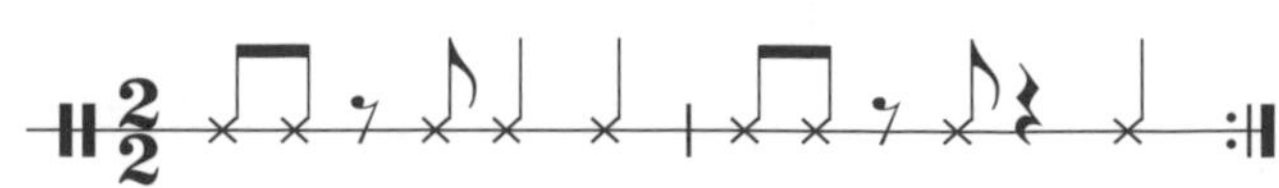

Improv Tools

Idea & Variation is another Improv Tool you can use, in addition to the **Sequence** and **Call & Response**.

Sequence: play an idea and then repeat it transposed to start on a different note:

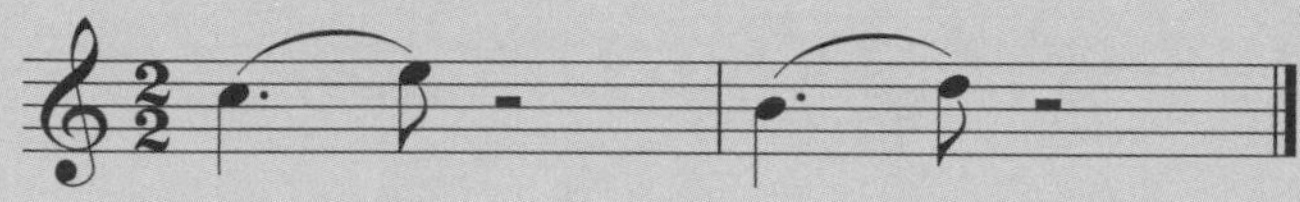

Call & Response: play an idea, then "answer" it with a contrasting idea:

Idea & Variation: play an idea and then repeat it slightly varied (even by as little as one note!):

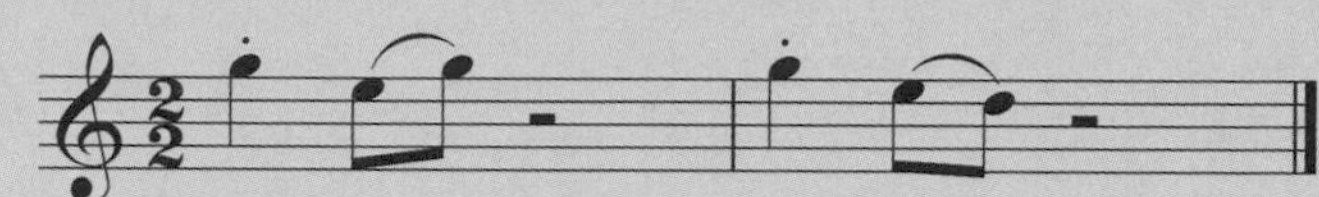

C Using the Improv Notes Set A or B as indicated in the score, play various right hand improvisations. Use the Improv Tools, above and in the previous Module, to get started. Practice *with* the backing track.

Set A
Improv notes:

Set B
Improv notes:

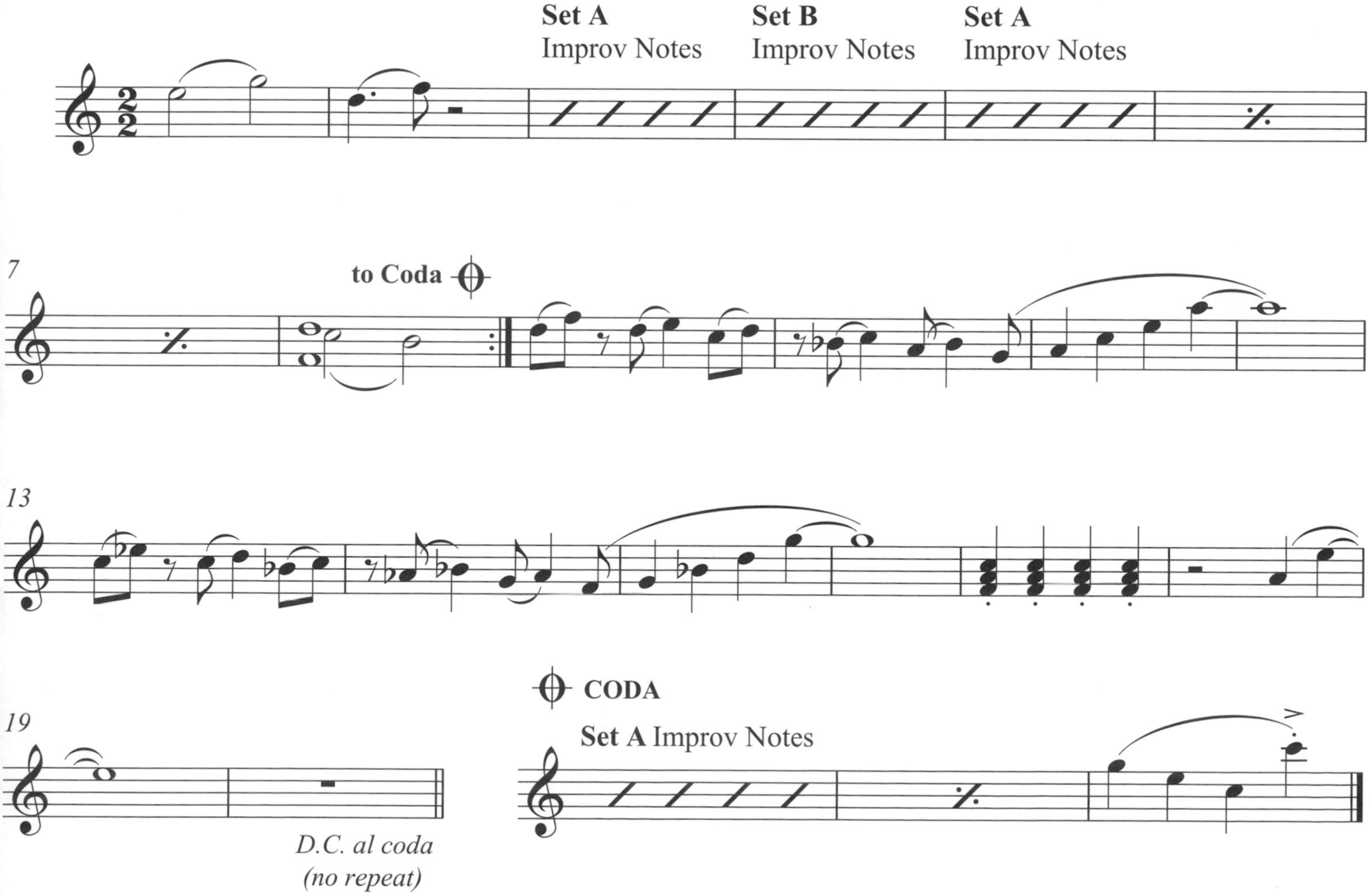

Set A Improv Notes — **Set B** Improv Notes — **Set A** Improv Notes

7 **to Coda**

13

19

D.C. al coda
(no repeat)

CODA

Set A Improv Notes

D Now improvise hands together. Practice first *without*, then *with* the backing track.

✔ **Improv Tip:** *Practice the left hand chord changes until they're automatic before you try to do too much with the right hand.*

Vamping Tools

Even though *Up and About* is very fast, you can still use broken chords, blocked chords, or a combination of both in your vamp.

Vamp Idea 1:

Idea 2:

Idea 3:

E Vamp various right hand accompaniments using the chords [in brackets] indicated below. Use the Vamping Tools, above and in the previous Module, to get started. Practice first *without*, then *with* the backing track.

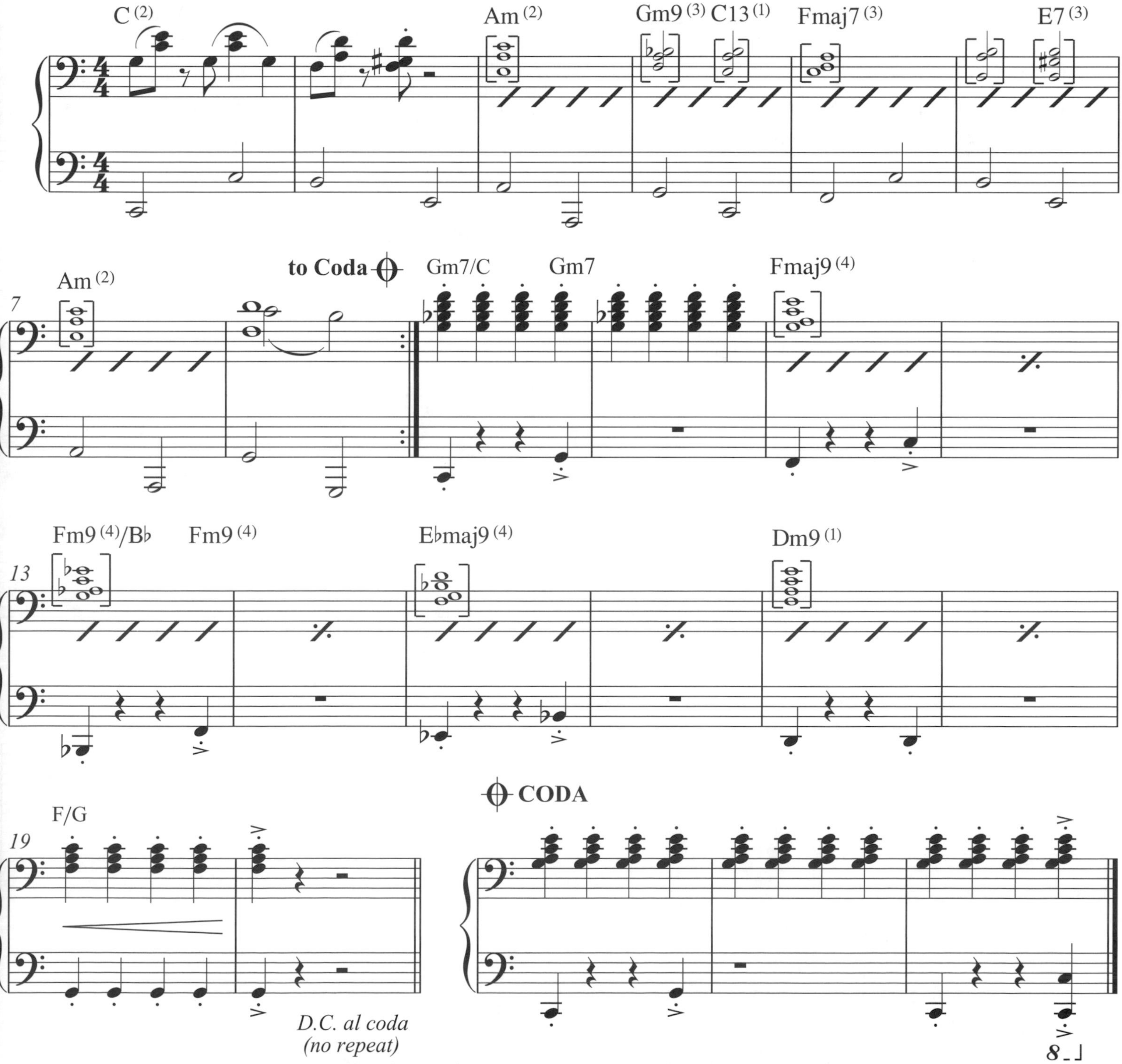

C (2) — Am (2) — Gm9 (3) C13 (1) — Fmaj7 (3) — E7 (3)

7 Am (2) — **to Coda** 𝄌 — Gm7/C — Gm7 — Fmaj9 (4)

13 Fm9 (4)/B♭ — Fm9 (4) — E♭maj9 (4) — Dm9 (1)

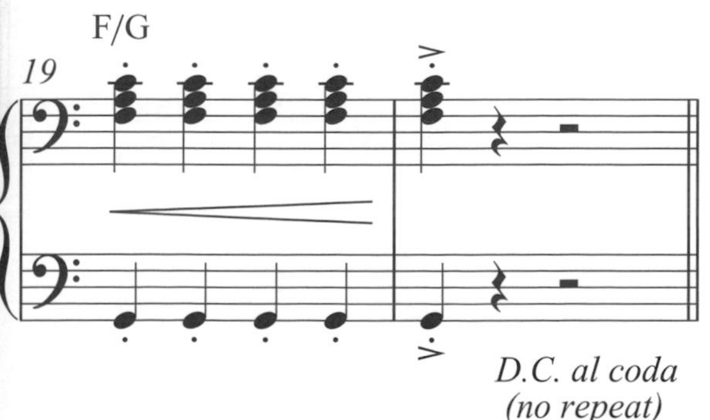

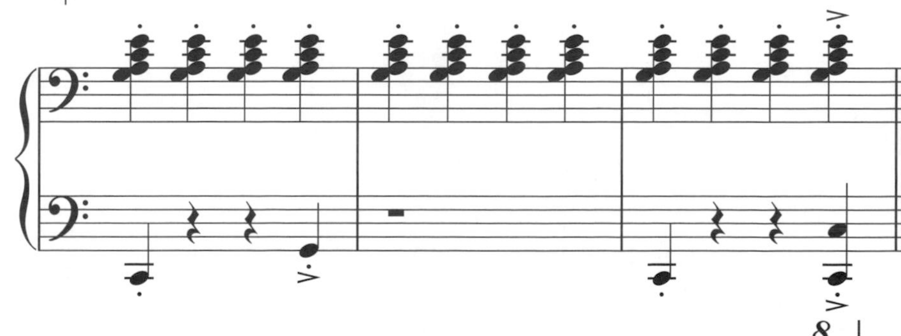

Improv Etude - Up and About

Module 3

Concept: major 6 & 7sus4 chords

A **major 6 chord** (also known as a 6 chord) combines a major triad (e.g., C-E-G) with a major 6th above the root (e.g., A). A suspension **7sus4 chord** (also known as a **7sus chord**), is created when the fourth degree of a scale is used in a 7 chord instead of the third degree, "suspending" the resolution we expect to hear.

6 chords may be written in **second inversion**. In a second inversion 6 chord, the fifth of the chord is on the bottom. 7sus chords may be written in **third inversion**.

C(2)
C6(2)
G7(3)
G7sus(3)
G7sus(3)
Second Inv.
Second Inv.
Third Inv.
Third Inv.
Third Inv. with no root

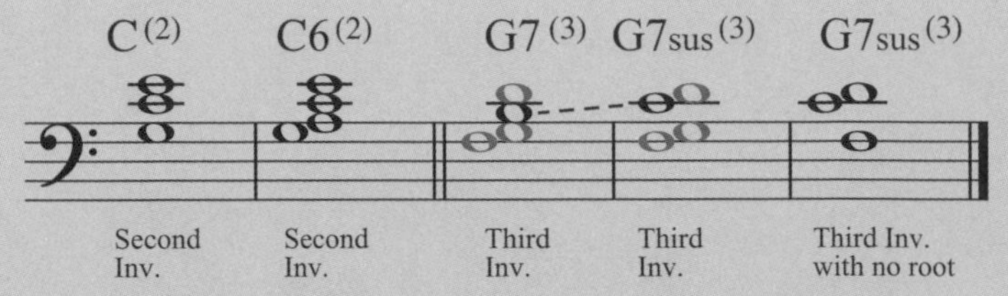

To review changing root position chords to second and third inversion, see Module 1 of *Sparkling* (pg. 14) and Module 2 of *Barbican Blues* (pg. 6).

For improvising on *Up and About*, the root of the 7sus chords will be played in the backing track.

A Label the second inversion 6 and third inversion 7sus chords with their lettername (e.g., C6 or G7sus) and a bracketed "2" or "3" for the correct inversion. Practice the left hand first *without*, then *with* the backing track.

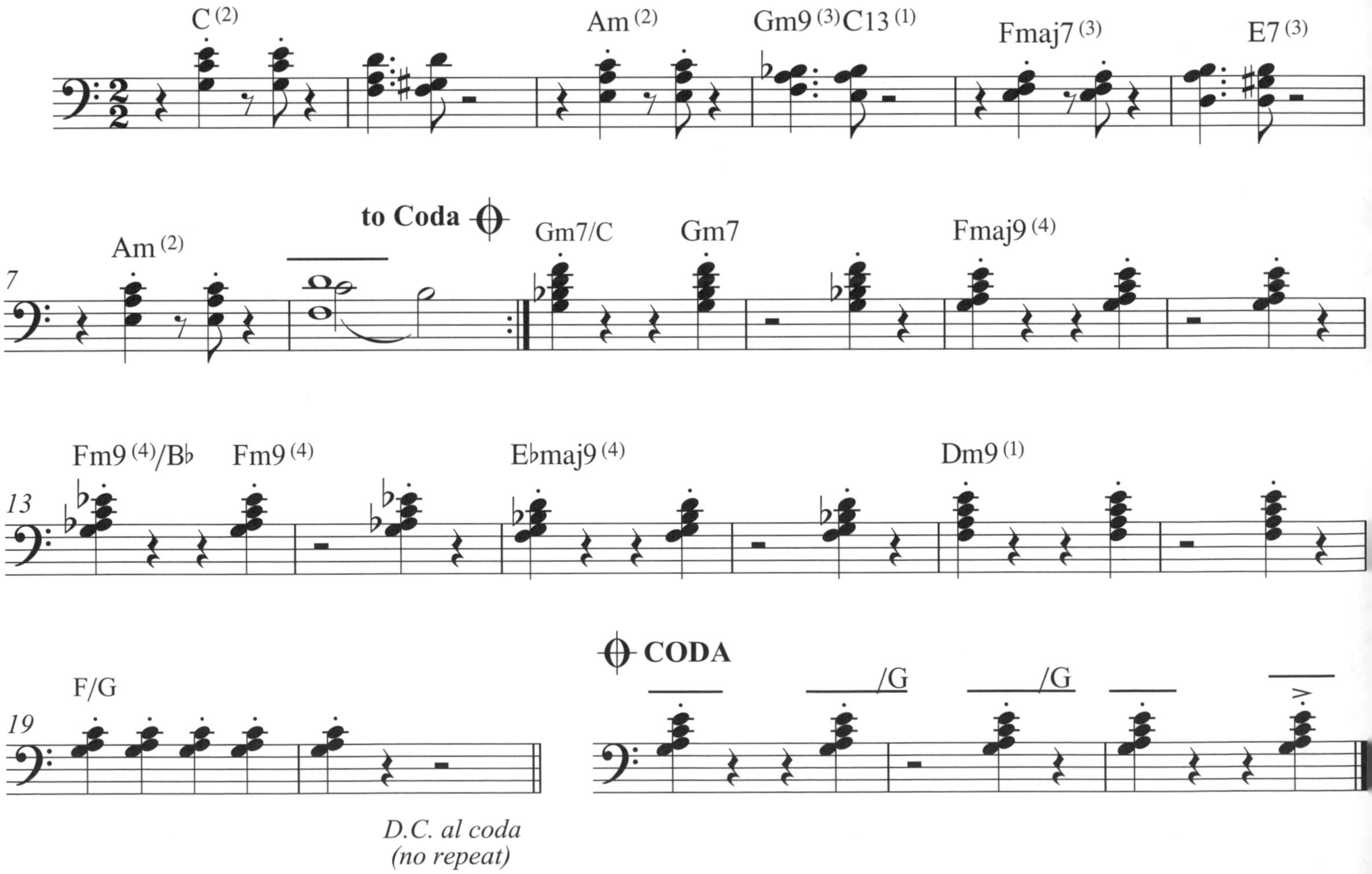
C(2)
Am(2)
Gm9(3)C13(1)
Fmaj7(3)
E7(3)
7
Am(2)
to Coda
Gm7/C
Gm7
Fmaj9(4)
13
Fm9(4)/B♭
Fm9(4)
E♭maj9(4)
Dm9(1)
19
F/G
CODA
/G
/G
D.C. al coda
(no repeat)

B Tap this rhythm while counting out loud; repeat until memorized. Then tap the rhythm with your right hand while playing the chord progression with your left. Finally, make up your own rhythms to go with the left hand chord progression.

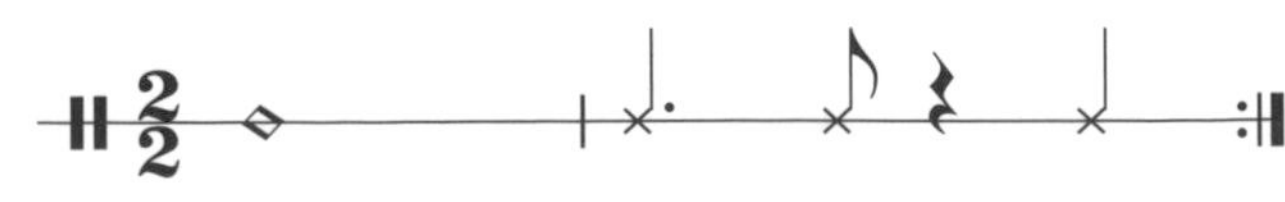

Improv Tools

There are other Improv Tools you can use to make your improvisation ideas more interesting and musical.

Direction Change: play an idea and then change its direction:

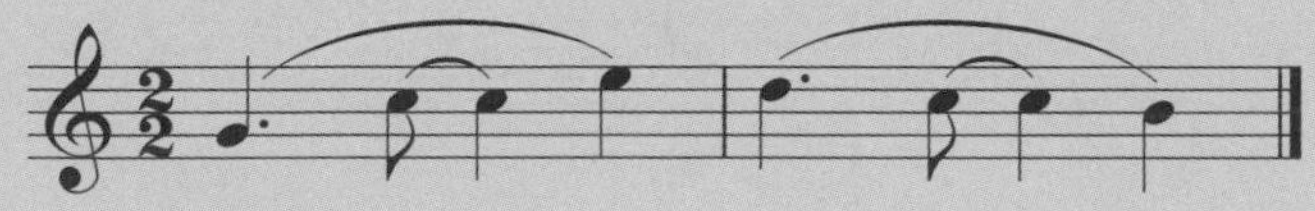

Grace Notes: grace notes can really "spice up" your ideas:

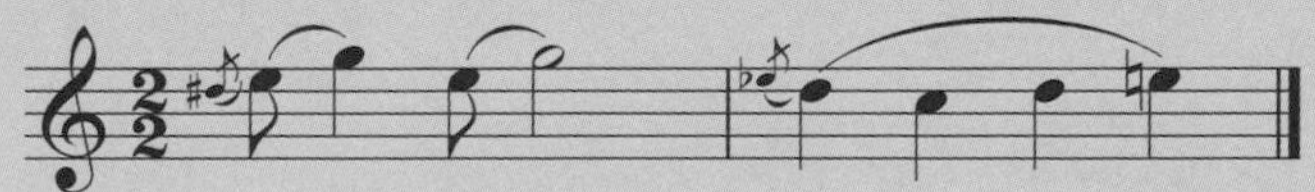

Thirds: play your musical idea in thirds to add further expressiveness to a melody:

C Using the Improv Notes Set A or B as indicated in the score, play various right hand improvisations. Use the Improv Tools, above and in the previous Modules, to get started. Practice *with* the backing track.

Set A
Improv notes:

Set B
Improv notes:

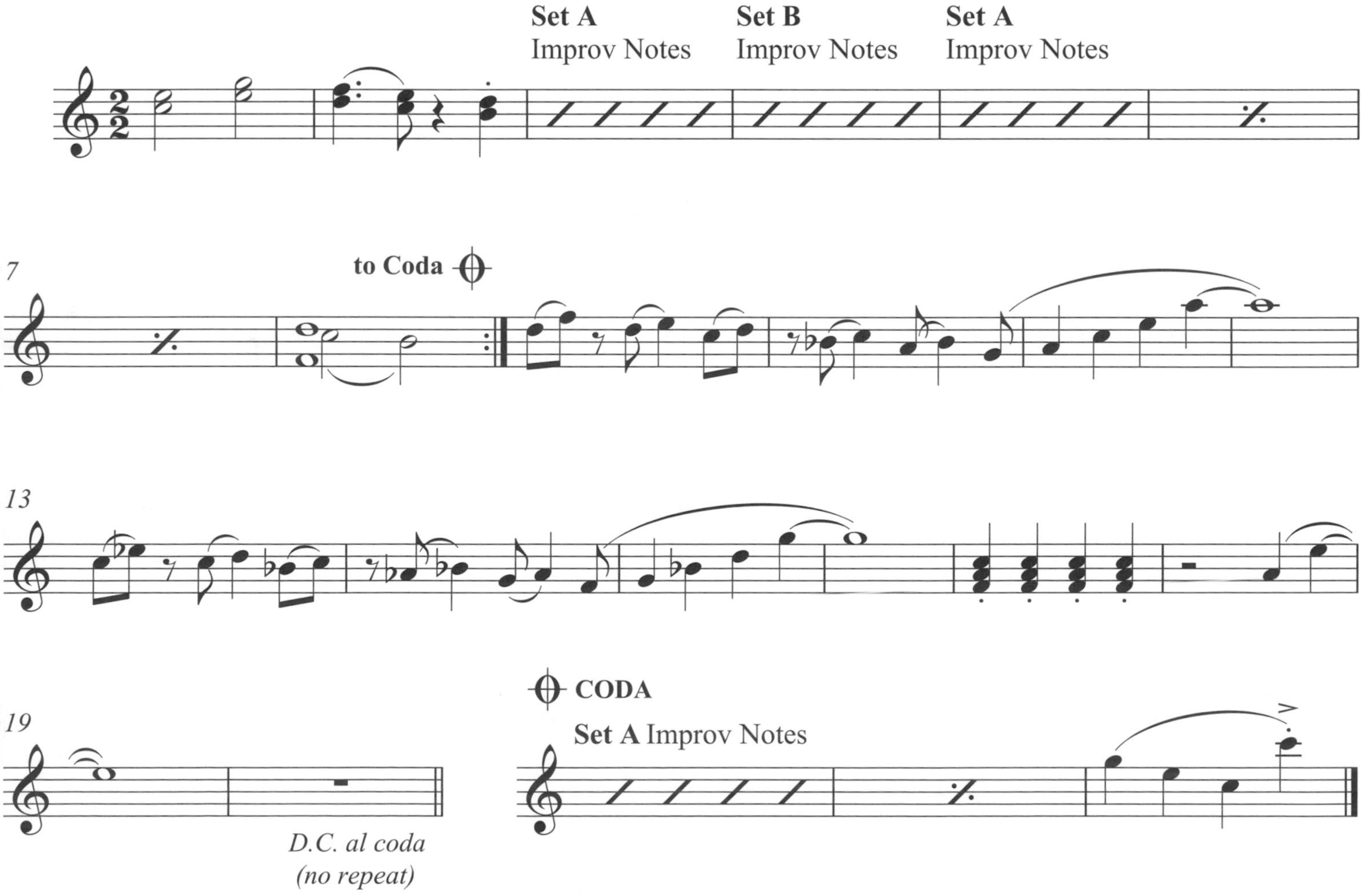

Set A Improv Notes | **Set B** Improv Notes | **Set A** Improv Notes

7

to Coda

13

19

D.C. al coda
(no repeat)

CODA

Set A Improv Notes

D Now improvise hands together. Practice first *without*, then *with* the backing track.

Improv Tip: *You don't always have to be playing a "solo". Try "laying back" and enjoy Chording, playing chords in both hands, as part of the rhythm section.*

Vamping Tools

Vamps can use a mixture of blocked and broken chords in the right hand. You can create interest in various ways:

Vamp Idea 1 – broken-up chord patterns:

Idea 2 – arpeggios:

Idea 3 – blocked chords and arpeggios:

E Vamp various right hand accompaniments using the chords [in brackets] indicated below. Use the Vamping Tools, above and in the previous Modules, to get started. Practice first *without*, then *with* the backing track.

C (2) | Am (2) | Gm9 (3) C13 (1) | Fmaj7 (3) | E7 (3)

7 Am (2) | G7sus (3) G7 (3) | **to Coda** 𝄌 Gm7/C | Gm7 | Fmaj9 (4)

13 Fm9 (4)/B♭ Fm9 (4) | E♭maj9 (4) | Dm9 (1)

19 F/G

D.C. al coda (no repeat)

𝄌 **CODA**

C6 (2) | C6 (2)/G | C6 (2)

8

Improv Etude - A Night in Lima

Module 1

Concept: minor 7 & minor 9 chords

A **minor 7 chord (m7)** combines a minor triad (e.g., F-A♭-C) with a minor 7th above the root (e.g., E♭). Minor 7 chords may be the top chord in a **split chord**. To review split chords, see Module 2 of *Sparkling* (pg. 18).

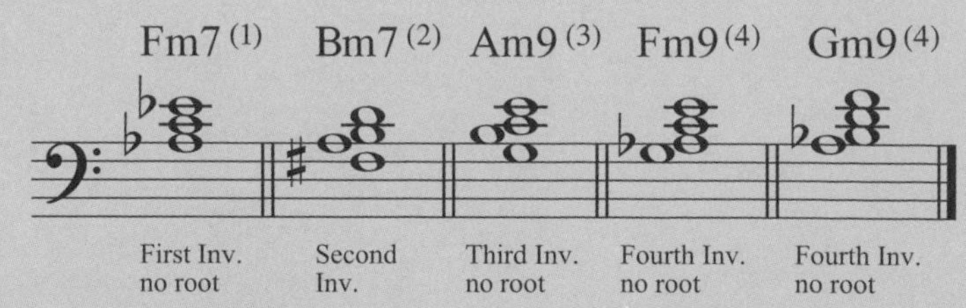

A **minor 9 chord (m9)** adds a major 9th (e.g., A) above the root to the m7 chord. Minor 9 chords may be written in **fourth inversion**. In a fourth inversion chord, the ninth of the chord is on the bottom. One way to change a root postion m9 chord to fourth inversion is to take the 9th off the top and put it on the bottom; you'll also lose the root or move it up an octave. To review first, second and third inversion, see Module 1 of *Barbican Blues* (pg. 2) and *Sparkling* (pg. 14), and Module 3 of *A Day on the Beach* (pg. 34).

In the *A Night in Lima* improvisation, the root of the m7 and m9 chords is played in the backing track.

A Label the m7, m7 split, and m9 chords with their lettername (e.g., Fm7, Bm7/A, Am9, Fm9, or Gm9) and a bracketed "1", "2", "3", or "4" for the inversion. Practice the left hand *without*, then *with* the backing track.

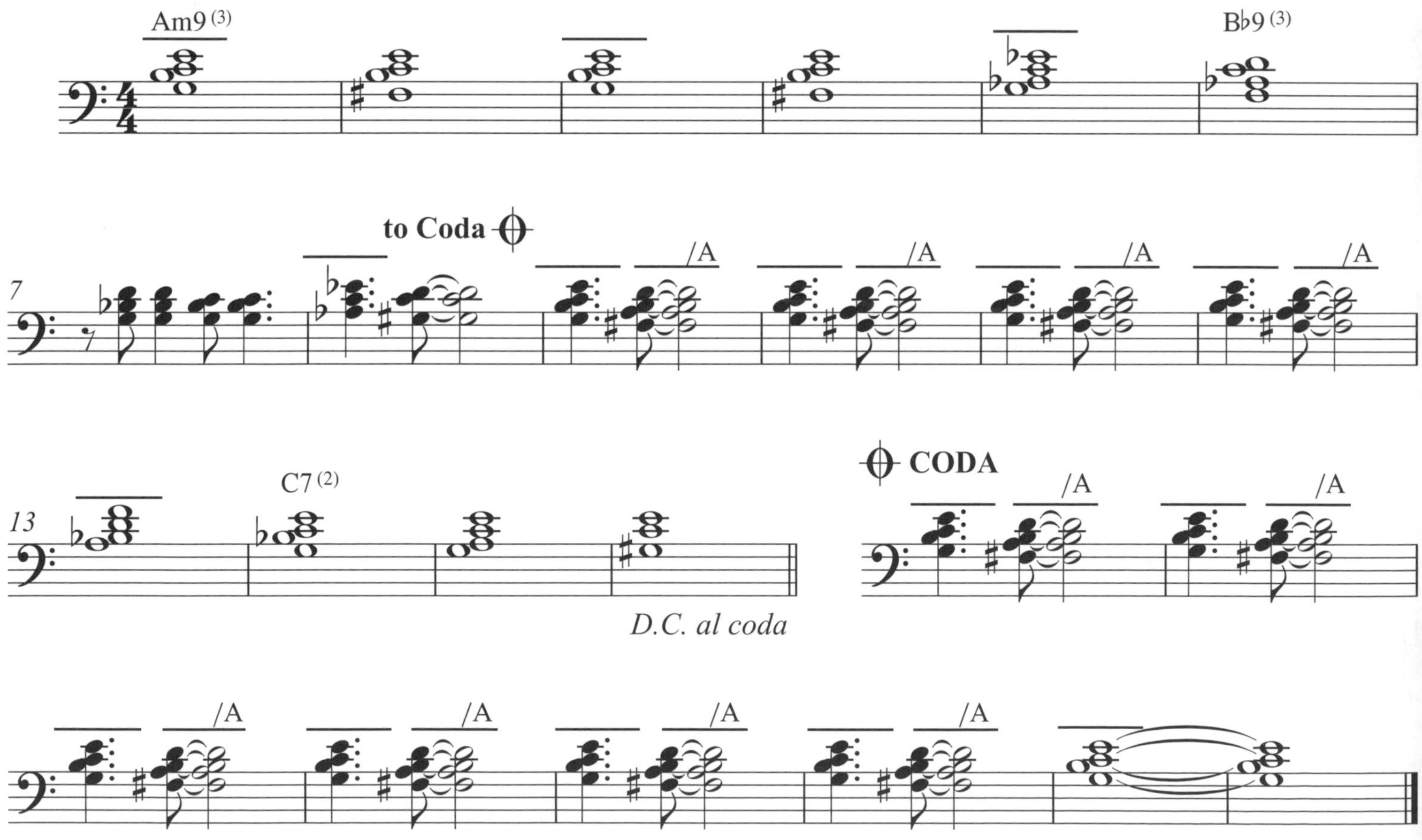

Am9 (3)
B♭9 (3)

to Coda
/A /A /A /A

C7 (2)

D.C. al coda

CODA
/A /A

/A /A /A /A

B Tap this rhythm while counting out loud; repeat until memorized. Then tap the rhythm with your right hand while playing the chord progression with your left. Finally, make up your own rhythms to go with the left hand chord progression.

Improv Tools

To improvise on *A Night in Lima*, you will use three sets of Improv Notes: based on the **A Dorian mode**, the **A♭ Lydian mode**, and the **A Phrygian mode**.

One way to describe A♭ Lydian is as an A♭ Major scale with a D♮ instead of a D♭. One way to describe A Phrygian is as an A natural minor scale with a B♭ instead of a B♮. To review the Dorian mode, check the Glossary (pg. 86).

There are Improv Tools you can use to make your improvisation interesting and musical.

Sequence: play a scale-based idea and then repeat it transposed to start on a different note:

Idea & Variation: play an idea and then repeat it slightly varied:

C Using the Improv Notes Set A, B, or C as indicated in the score, play various right hand improvisations. Use the Improv Tools, above, to get started. Practice *with* the backing track.

Set A Improv notes: **Set B** Improv notes:  **Set C** Improv notes:

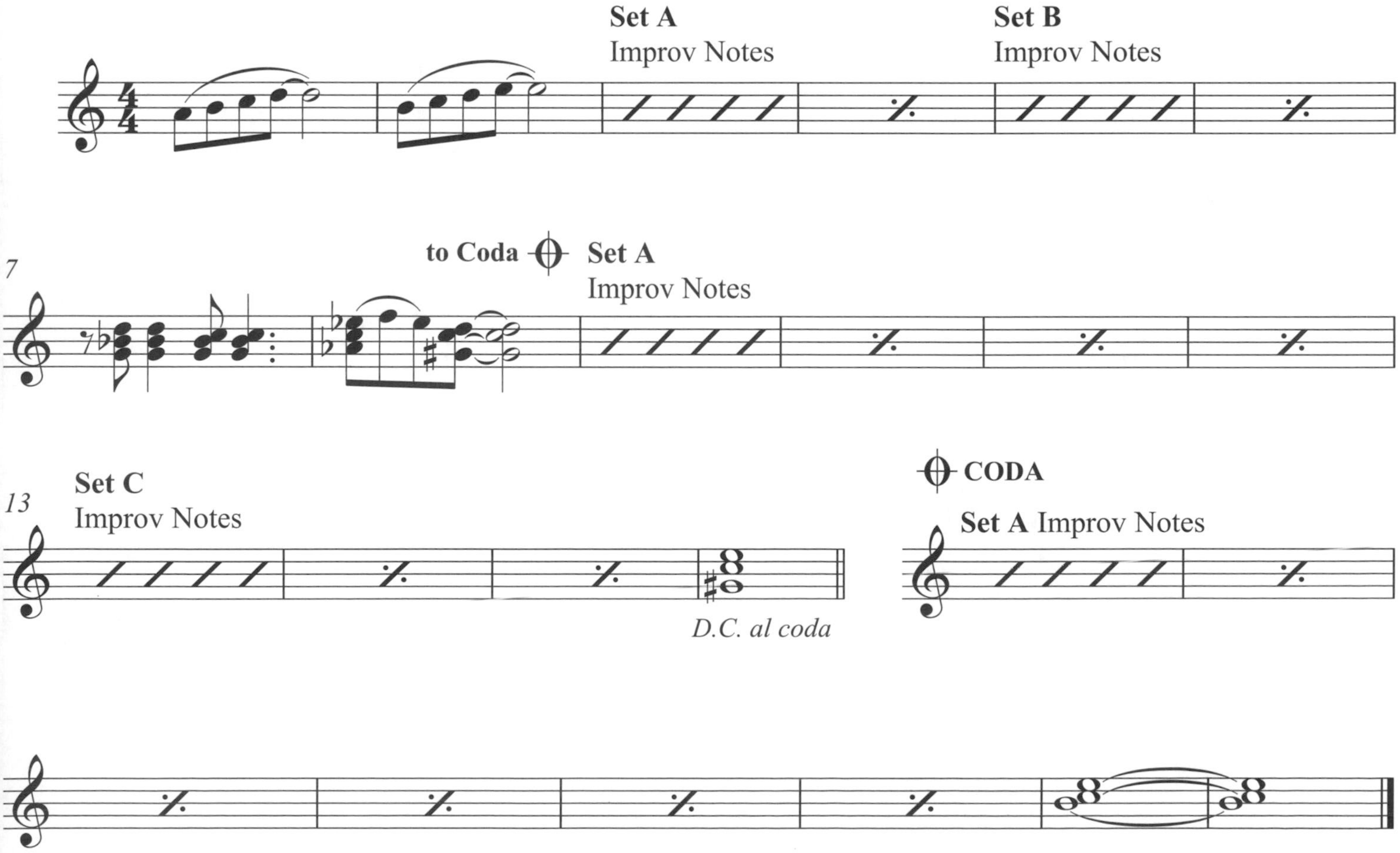

Set A Improv Notes **Set B** Improv Notes

7 to Coda **Set A** Improv Notes

13 **Set C** Improv Notes

D.C. al coda

CODA **Set A** Improv Notes

D Now improvise hands together. Practice first *without*, then *with* the backing track.

Set A Improv notes:

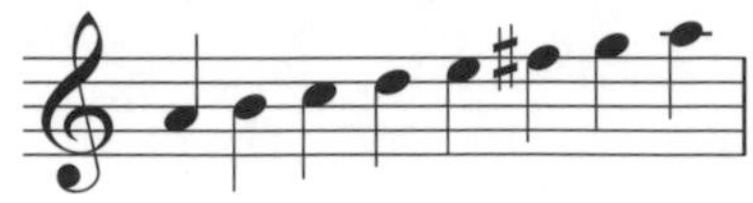

Set B Improv notes:

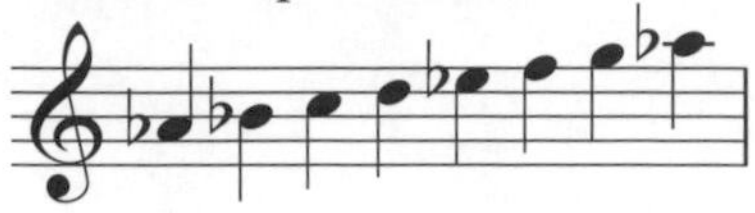

Set C Improv notes:

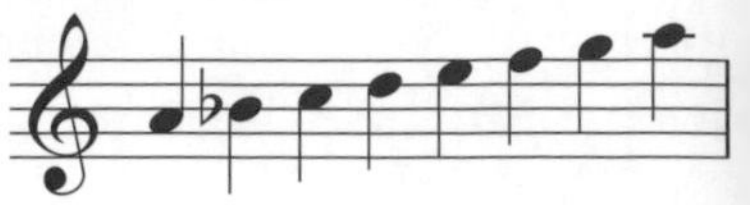

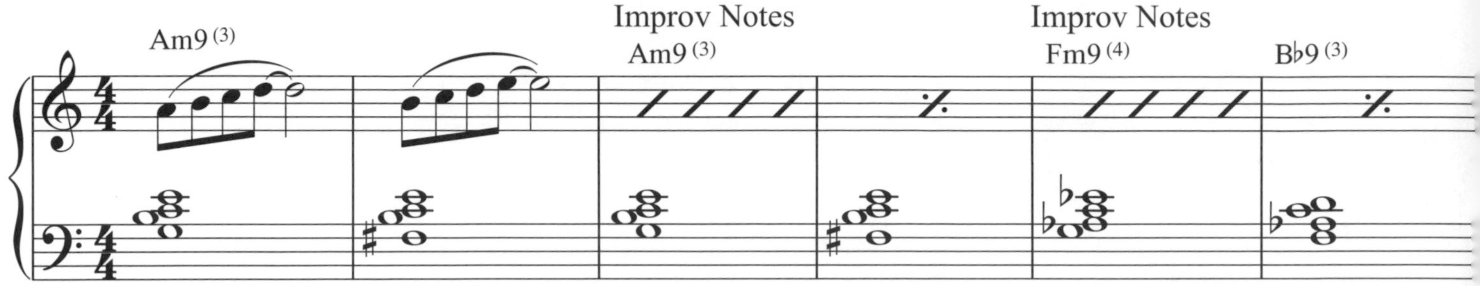

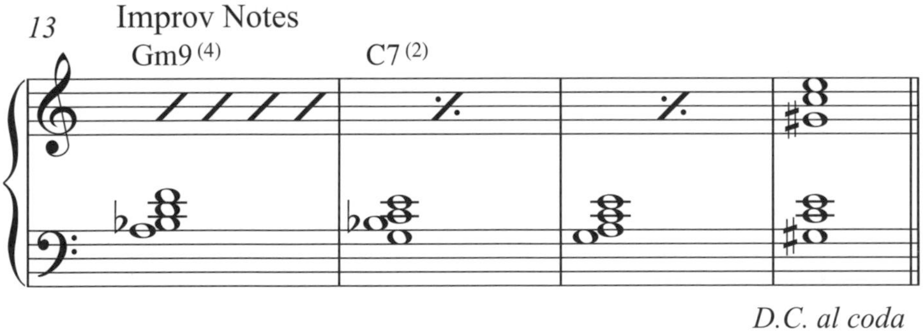

Am9 (3)

Set A
Improv Notes
Am9 (3)

Set B
Improv Notes
Fm9 (4) B♭9 (3)

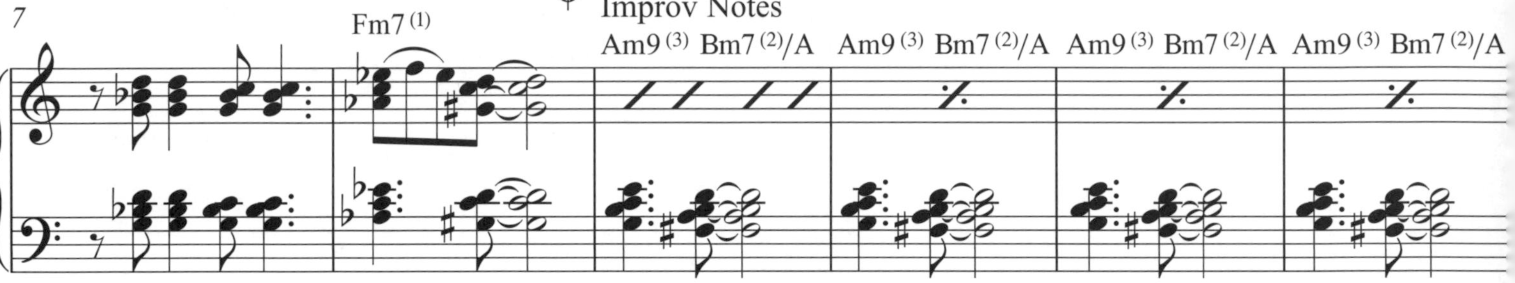

7

Fm7 (1)

to Coda 𝄌 **Set A**
Improv Notes
Am9 (3) Bm7 (2)/A Am9 (3) Bm7 (2)/A Am9 (3) Bm7 (2)/A Am9 (3) Bm7 (2)/A

Set C
Improv Notes
Gm9 (4) C7 (2)

D.C. al coda

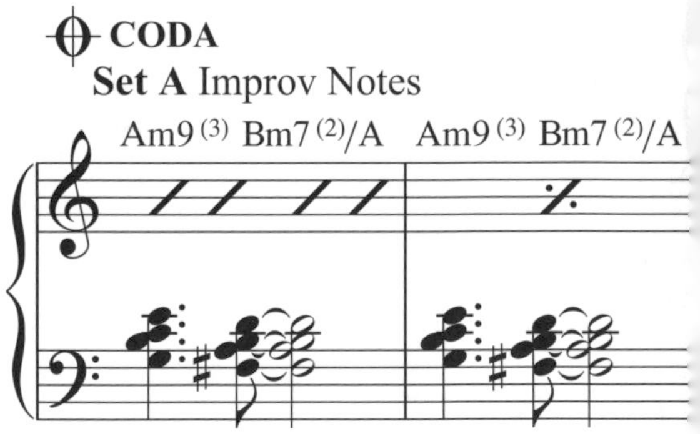

𝄌 **CODA**
Set A Improv Notes
Am9 (3) Bm7 (2)/A Am9 (3) Bm7 (2)/A

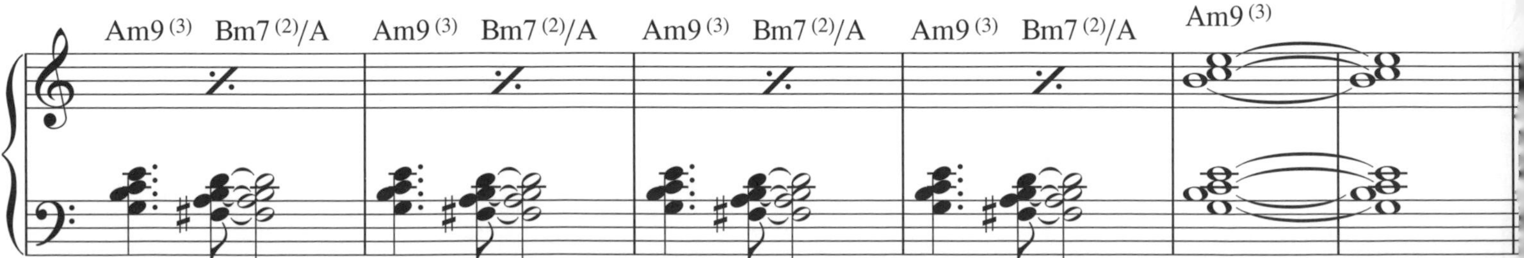

✔ **Improv Tip:** *With three similar, but distinct Improv Notes Sets, make sure you know which notes they have in common and which notes are different.*

Vamping Tools

Vamping is an improvised accompaniment, often with chords in the right hand against single notes in the left. You can vary blocked right hand chords by changing the pattern of the rhythms.

Vamp Idea 1 – based on the left hand rhythm:

Idea 2 – a more syncopated right hand rhythm:

Idea 3 – a combination of Ideas 1 & 2:

E Vamp various right hand accompaniments using the chords [in brackets] indicated below. Use the Vamping Tools, above, to get started. Practice first *without*, then *with* the backing track.

Am9 (3) Am9 (3) Fm9 (4) B♭9 (3)

7 Fm7 (1) **to Coda** Am9 (3) Bm7 (2)/A Am9 (3) Bm7 (2)/A Am9 (3) Bm7 (2)/A Am9 (3) Bm7 (2)/A

13 Gm9 (4) C7 (2)

D.C. al coda

CODA Am9 (3) Bm7 (2)/A Am9 (3) Bm7 (2)/A

Am9 (3) Bm7 (2)/A Am9 (3) Bm7 (2)/A Am9 (3) Bm7 (2)/A Am9 (3) Bm7 (2)/A Am9 (3)

Improv Etude - A Night in Lima

Module 2

Concept: major 7 & major 9 chords

A **major 7 chord (maj7)** combines a major triad (e.g., E♭-G-B♭) with a major 7th above the root (e.g., D). This is the same construction as the 7 chord, only using a major 7th instead of a minor 7th. Similarly, a **major 9 chord (maj9)** adds a 9th above the root to the maj7 chord (e.g., F-A-C-E-G).

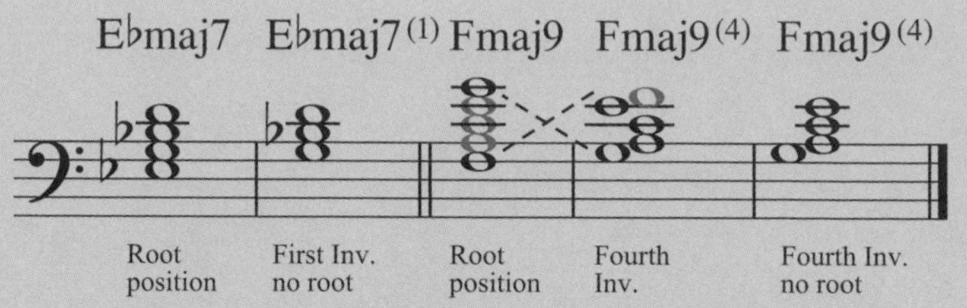

Major 9 chords may be written in **fourth inversion**. In a fourth inversion chord, the ninth of the chord is on the bottom. One way to change a root postion maj9 chord to fourth inversion is to take the 9th off the top and put it on the bottom; you'll also lose the root or move it up an octave. To review first inversion, see Module 1 of *Barbican Blues* (pg. 2).

E♭maj7
E♭maj7(1)
Fmaj9
Fmaj9(4)
Fmaj9(4)
Root position
First Inv. no root
Root position
Fourth Inv.
Fourth Inv. no root

In the *A Night in Lima* improvisation, the root of the maj7(1) and maj9(4) chords is played in the backing track.

A Label the maj7 and maj9 chords with their lettername (e.g., E♭maj7 or Fmaj9) and a bracketed "1"or"4" for the inversion as appropriate. Practice the left hand first *without*, then *with* the backing track.

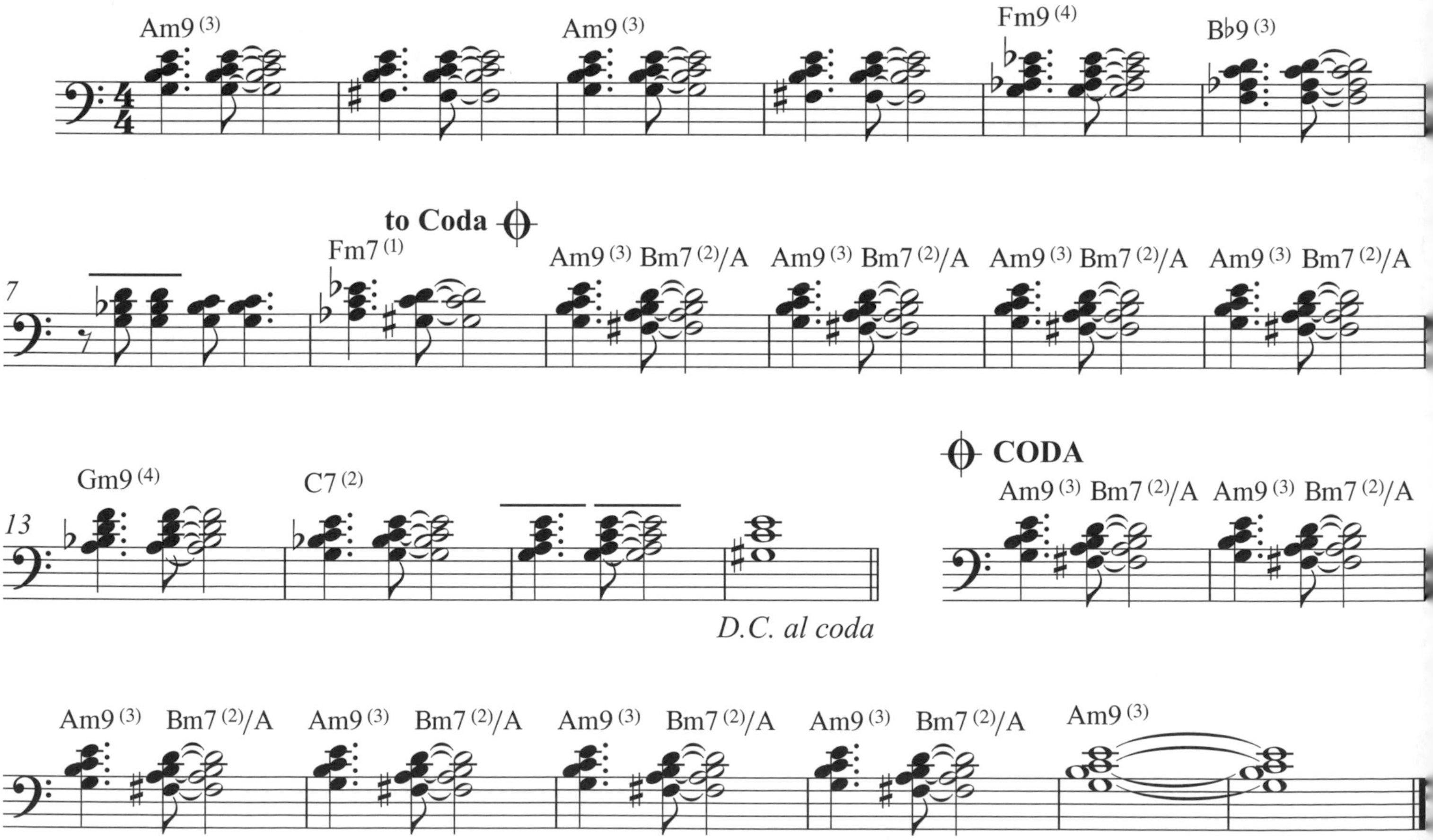

Am9(3)
Am9(3)
Fm9(4)
B♭9(3)
to Coda
Fm7(1)
Am9(3) Bm7(2)/A
Am9(3) Bm7(2)/A
Am9(3) Bm7(2)/A
Am9(3) Bm7(2)/A
Gm9(4)
C7(2)
D.C. al coda
CODA
Am9(3) Bm7(2)/A Am9(3) Bm7(2)/A
Am9(3) Bm7(2)/A
Am9(3) Bm7(2)/A
Am9(3) Bm7(2)/A
Am9(3) Bm7(2)/A
Am9(3)

B Tap this rhythm while counting out loud; repeat until memorized. Then tap the rhythm with your right hand while playing the chord progression with your left. Finally, make up your own rhythms to go with the left hand chord progression.

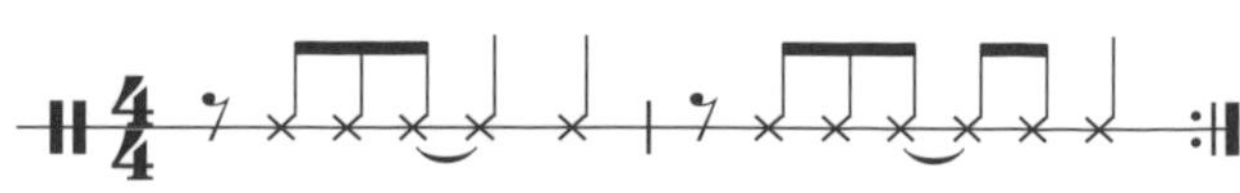

Improv Tools

Call & Response is another Improv Tool you can use, in addition to **Sequence** and **Idea & Variation**.

You can also use arpeggio-based ideas.

Sequence: play an arpeggio-based idea and then repeat the shape of the idea starting on a different note:

Idea & Variation: play an arpeggio-based idea and then repeat it slightly varied (even by as little as one note!):

Call & Response: create an arpeggio-based idea, then "answer" it with a contrasting idea:

C Using the Improv Notes Set A, B, or C as indicated in the score, play various right hand improvisations. Use the Improv Tools, above and in the previous Module, to get started. Practice *with* the backing track.

Set A Improv notes:

Set B Improv notes:

Set C Improv notes:

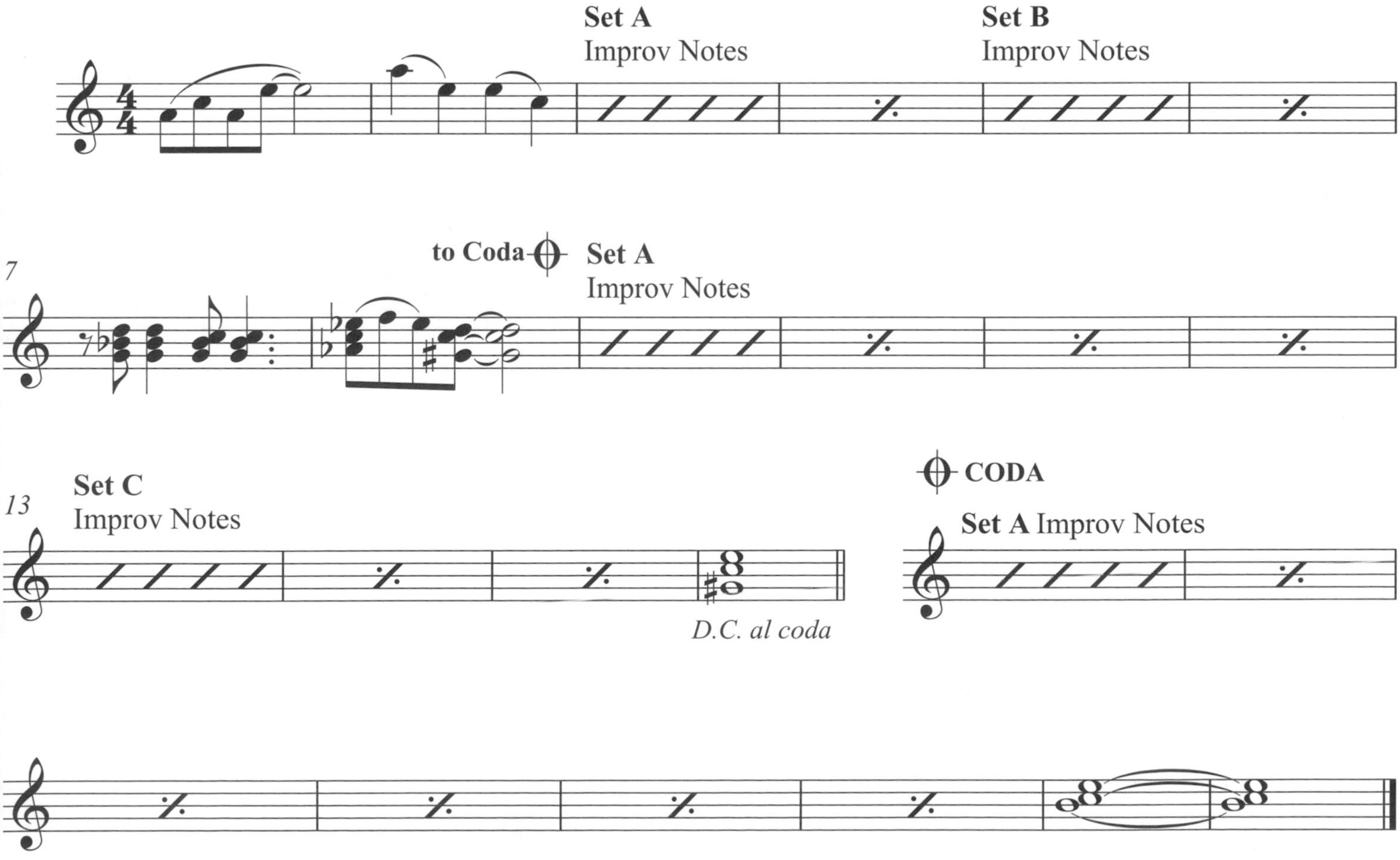

Set A Improv Notes

Set B Improv Notes

7

to Coda

Set A Improv Notes

13

Set C Improv Notes

D.C. al coda

CODA

Set A Improv Notes

D Now improvise hands together. Practice first *without*, then *with* the backing track.

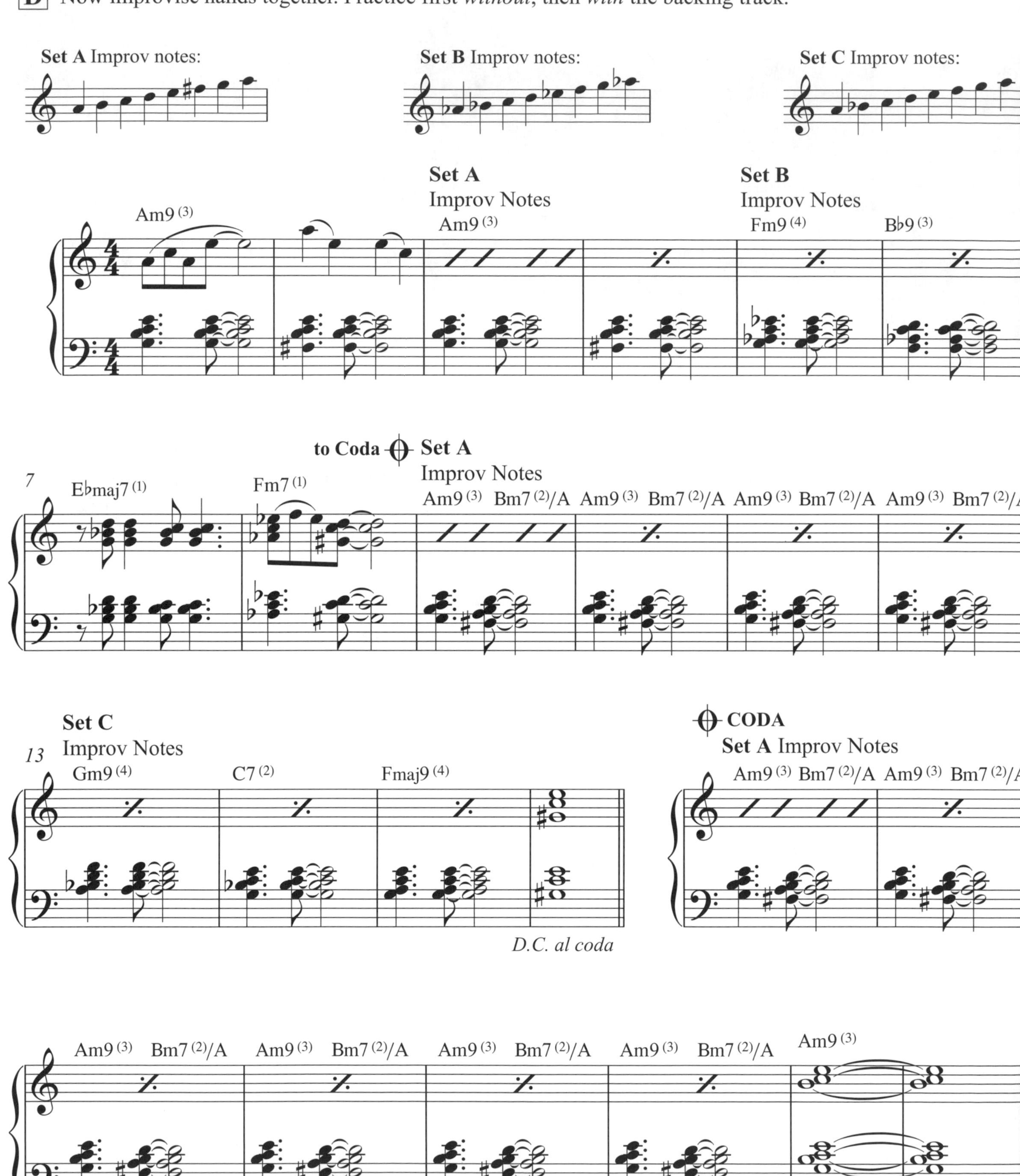

✔ **Improv Tip:** *Try this for an Idea & Variation: use the written melody as the idea and do a variation on it in your improvisation.*

Vamping Tools

There are several ways to vary broken chords in your vamp.

Vamp Idea 1 – starting on the bottom note of the chord:

Idea 2 – starting on the top note of the chord:

Idea 3 – a variation of Idea 2:

E Vamp various right hand accompaniments using the chords [in brackets] indicated below. Use the Vamping Tools, above and in the previous Module, to get started. Practice first *without*, then *with* the backing track.

Am9 (3) | | Am9 (3) | | Fm9 (4) | B♭9 (3)

7 E♭maj7 (1) | Fm7 (1) **to Coda** | Am9 (3) Bm7 (2)/A | Am9 (3) Bm7 (2)/A | Am9 (3) Bm7 (2)/A | Am9 (3) Bm7 (2)/A

13 Gm9 (4) | C7 (2) | Fmaj9 (4) |

D.C. al coda

CODA

Am9 (3) Bm7 (2)/A | Am9 (3) Bm7 (2)/A

Am9 (3) Bm7 (2)/A | Am9 (3) Bm7 (2)/A | Am9 (3) Bm7 (2)/A | Am9 (3) Bm7 (2)/A | Am9 (3)

Improv Etude - A Night in Lima

Module 3

Concept: augmented & minor 6add9 chords

Am6
Am6 (3)
Am6add9 (3)
Am6add9 (3)
Root position
Third Inversion
Third Inversion
Third Inversion no root or 5th

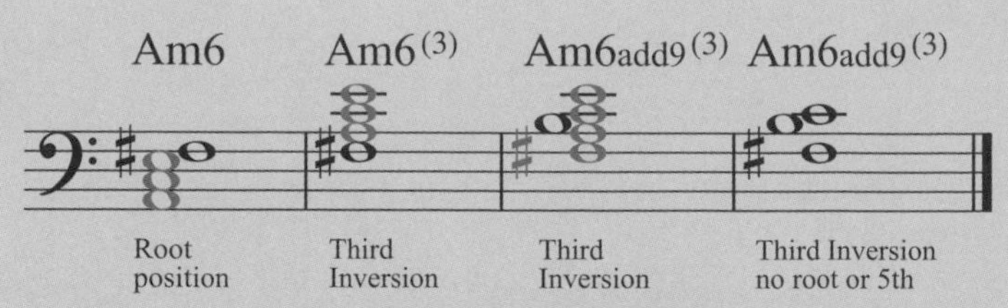

An **augmented chord (aug)** is a major chord with a raised 5th instead of a perfect 5th (e.g., E-G♯-C [B♯]). A 7 chord may also be augmented (e.g., E-G♯-C-D) and written in **first inversion**.

A **minor 6 chord (m6)** combines a minor triad (e.g., A-C-E) with a major 6th above the root (e.g., F♯). A 9 chord extends a dominant 7 chord by adding a major 9th above the root to the chord. When the 7th is to be left out, this is indicated by saying the 9th is "added". A **minor 6add9** chord (**m6add9**) adds a 9th, without the 7th, to the chord (e.g, A-C-E-F♯-B).

For improvising on *A Night in Lima*, the root of the m6add9 and 7aug chords will be played in the backing track.

A Label the m6add9 and 7aug chords with their lettername (e.g., E7aug or Am6add9) and a bracketed "1" or "3" for the correct inversion. Practice the left hand first *without*, then *with* the backing track.

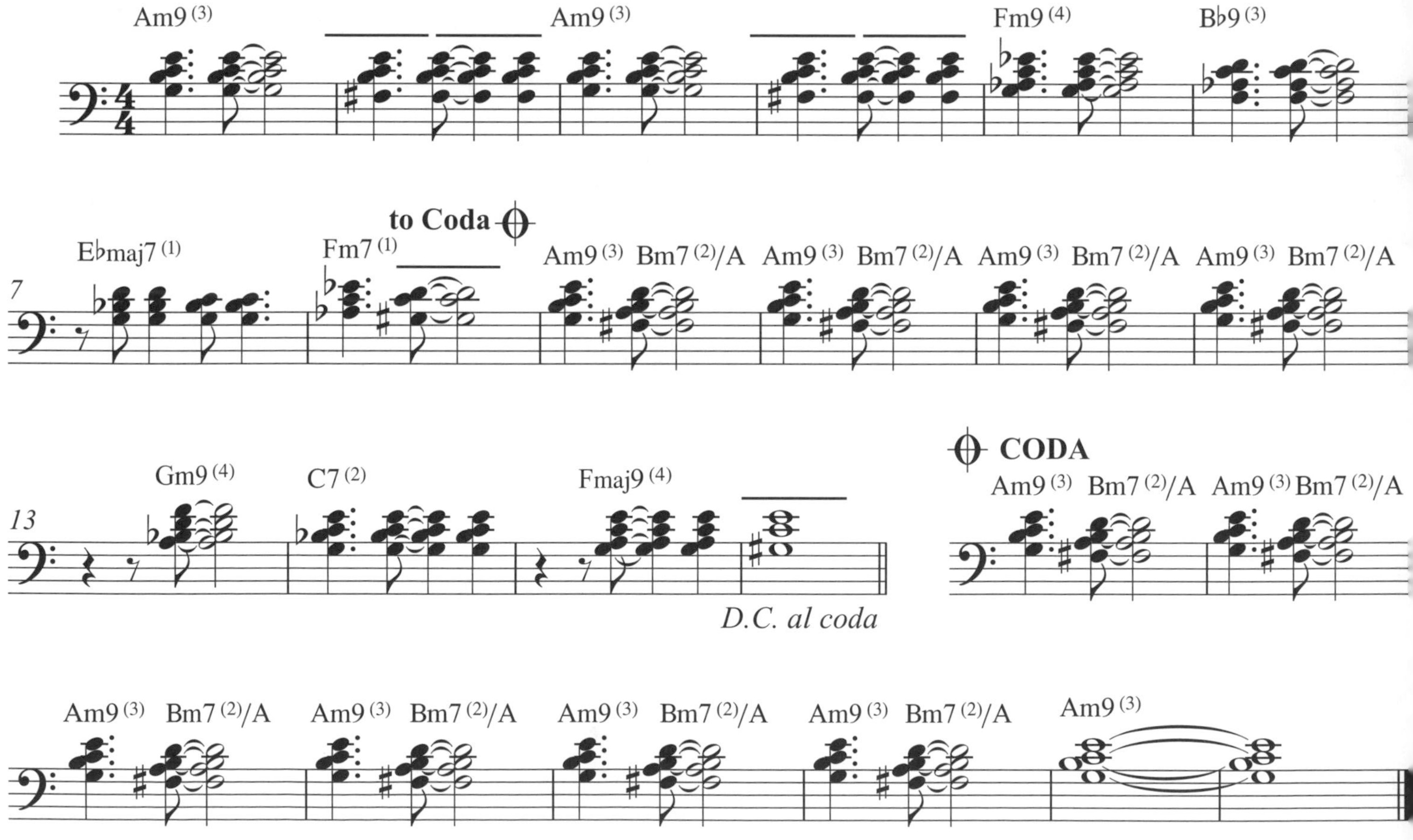

Am9 (3)
Am9 (3)
Fm9 (4)
B♭9 (3)
7
E♭maj7 (1)
to Coda
Fm7 (1)
Am9 (3) Bm7 (2)/A Am9 (3) Bm7 (2)/A Am9 (3) Bm7 (2)/A Am9 (3) Bm7 (2)/A
13
Gm9 (4)
C7 (2)
Fmaj9 (4)
D.C. al coda
CODA
Am9 (3) Bm7 (2)/A Am9 (3) Bm7 (2)/A
Am9 (3) Bm7 (2)/A Am9 (3) Bm7 (2)/A Am9 (3) Bm7 (2)/A Am9 (3) Bm7 (2)/A
Am9 (3)

B Tap this rhythm while counting out loud; repeat until memorized. Then tap the rhythm with your right hand while playing the chord progression with your left. Finally, make up your own rhythms to go with the left hand chord progression.

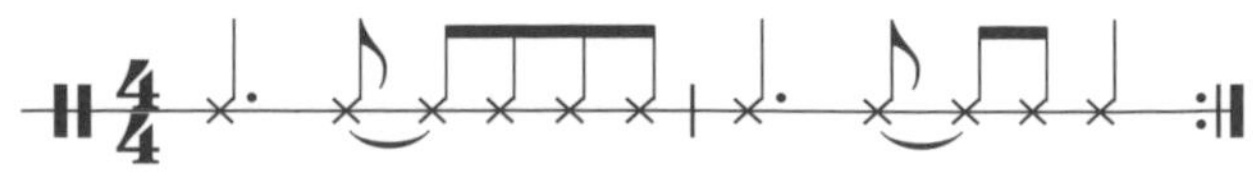

Improv Tools

There are other Improv Tools you can use, with either scale-based or arpeggio-based ideas, or a mixture of the two.

Rhythmic Shift: play an idea and then re-state it starting on a different beat:

Thirds & Fourths: create ideas that work in thirds or fourths to add character to a melody:

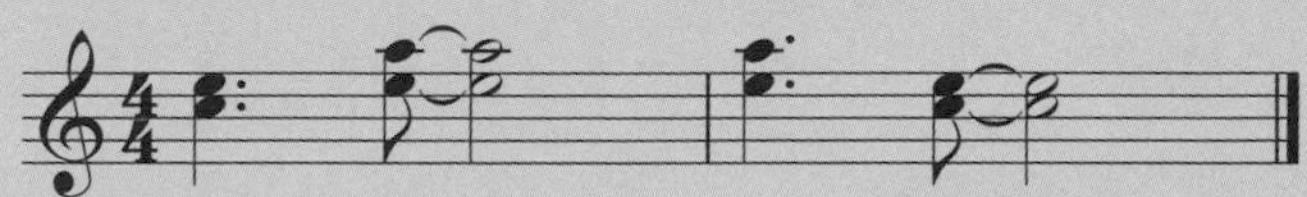

Grace Notes: subtle use of grace notes can make your improvisation more expressive:

C Using the Improv Notes Set A, B, or C as indicated in the score, play various right hand improvisations. Use the Improv Tools, above and in the previous Modules, to get started. Practice *with* the backing track.

Set A Improv notes:

Set B Improv notes:

Set C Improv notes:

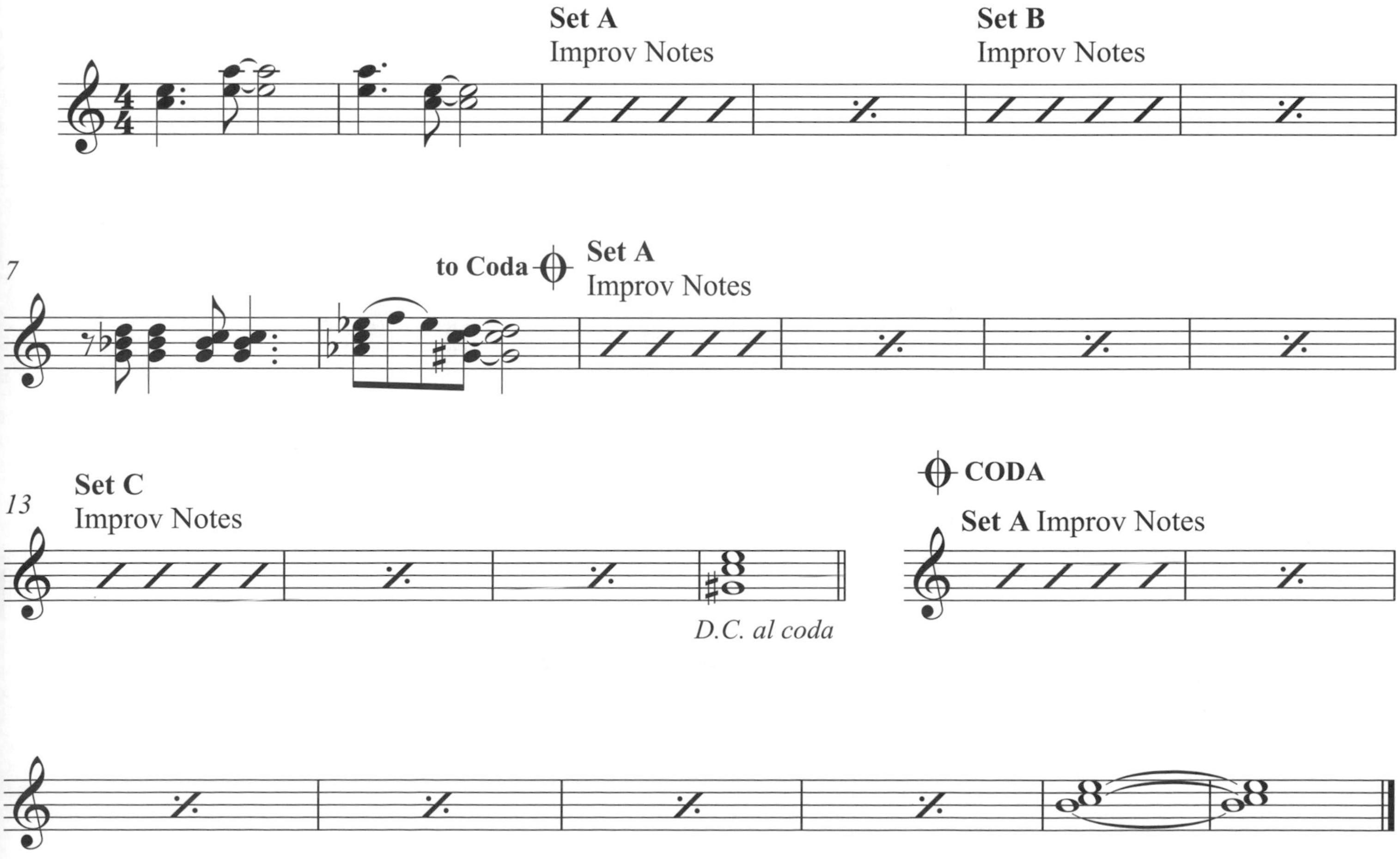

Set A Improv Notes

Set B Improv Notes

7

to Coda

Set A Improv Notes

13

Set C Improv Notes

D.C. al coda

CODA

Set A Improv Notes

D Now improvise hands together. Practice first *without*, then *with* the backing track.

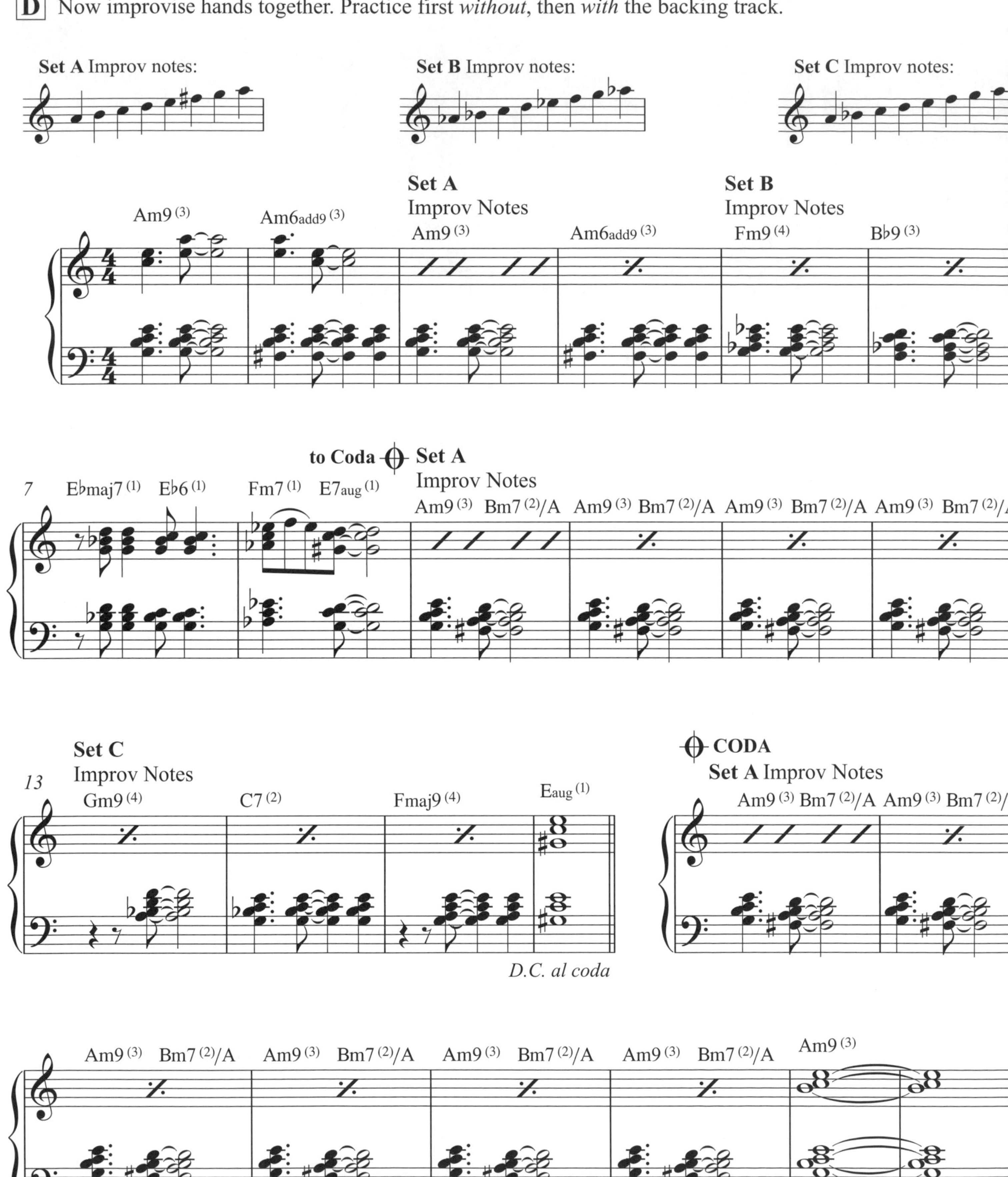

✔ **Improv Tip:** *Notice how effective syncopated left-hand chords can be in setting a certain mood. Experiment with using this technique in the right hand.*

Vamping Tools

Vamps can use a mixture of blocked and broken chords in the right hand. You can create interest by varying the mix, the arpeggios, or the rhythm:

Vamp Idea 1:

Idea 2:

Idea 3:

E Vamp various right hand accompaniments using the chords [in brackets] indicated below. Use the Vamping Tools, above and in the previous Modules, to get started. Practice first *without*, then *with* the backing track.

Am9 (3) Am6add9 (3) Am9 (3) Am6add9 (3) Fm9 (4) B♭9 (3)

7 E♭maj7 (1) E♭6 (1) Fm7 (1) E7aug (1) **to Coda** Am9 (3) Bm7 (2)/A Am9 (3) Bm7 (2)/A Am9 (3) Bm7 (2)/A Am9 (3) Bm7 (2)/A

13 Gm9 (4) C7 (2) Fmaj9 (4) Eaug (1)

D.C. al coda

CODA

Am9 (3) Bm7 (2)/A Am9 (3) Bm7 (2)/A

Am9 (3) Bm7 (2)/A Am9 (3) Bm7 (2)/A Am9 (3) Bm7 (2)/A Am9 (3) Bm7 (2)/A Am9 (3)

Poco Vivo

Stephen Heller

Poco Vivo ♩. = 84-92

cresc.

Allegretto

Louis Kohler

Allegretto

Henry Lemoine

Andante

Stephen Heller

Allegretto

Henri Bertini

Allegretto

Carl Czerny

In the Saddle

Christopher Norton

Bandstand

Christopher Norton

Punchy ♩ = 144

swung 8ths

mf

f

smoothly

Keep It Going

Christopher Norton

With pace ♩ = 132

swung 8s

17
3
1
4
3
mp

21
3
3
f

25

29
mf
mp
f
rh
8

Highwalk

Christopher Norton

Skyward

Christopher Norton

LEVEL 8 ETUDES

Glossary

Chord Structures

6 Chords ...... Chords which contain the sixth scale degree above the root.

major 6 ...... Combines a major triad (C-E-G) with the note a major sixth above the root (A). Notated: C6

minor 6 ...... Combines a minor triad (C-E♭-G) with the note a major sixth above the root (A). Notated: Cm6

7 Chords ...... Chords which contain either a major or minor seventh scale degree above the root.

dominant 7 .. Also known as a "7 chord". A major triad (C-E-G) combined with the note a minor 7th above the root (B♭). Notated: C7

major 7 ...... Combines a major triad (C-E-G) with the note a major seventh above the root (B). Notated: Cmaj7

minor 7 ...... A minor triad (C-E♭-G) combined with the note a minor seventh above the root (B♭). Notated: Cm7

9 Chords ...... Extended chords which contain the major ninth scale degree above the root

dominant 9 .. Also known as a "9 chord". A 7 chord (C-E-G-B♭) with an added major ninth on top (C-E-G-B♭-D). Notated: C9

major 9 ...... Adds a ninth above the root to the maj7 chord (C-E-G-B-D). Notated: Cmaj9

minor 9 ...... A minor 7 chord (C-E♭-G-B♭) with an added major ninth above the root (D). Notated: Cm9

13 Chords..... Extended chords which contain the major 13th scale degree above the root.

dominant 13 . Also known as a "13 chord". A 7 chord (C-E-G-B♭) with an added major 9th, 11th, and 13th above the root (D, F, A an octave above). Usually the 11th and sometimes the 9th are omitted. Notated: C13

Add Chords .. Indicates a note above the octave is added to a non-7 chord, without including every chord note in between. See Extended Chords.

add9.......... Starts with a triad (C-E-G) and adds the note a ninth above the root (D). Notated: Cadd9

m6add9....... Starts with a m6 chord (C-E♭-G-A) and adds a ninth above the root to the chord (D). Notated: Cm6add9

Augmented Chords ... A major chord in which the fifth is raised a half step (C-E-G♯). Notated: Caug

7aug.......... A 7 chord in which the fifth is raised a half step (C-E-G♯-B♭). Notated: C7aug

Close Position........... When the notes of a chord are arranged as close together as possible (C major triad played C-E-G).

Extended Chords...... Indicates a note or notes above the octave are added to a 7 chord; could include every chord note in between (9, 11, or 13 chords). See Added Chords.

Inversions..... Chords in which the root is not on the bottom.

first........... The third of a chord (the note E in a C major chord of C) is at the bottom of a chord (E-G-C). Notated: $C^{(1)}$

second .... The fifth of a chord (the note G in a C major chord of C) is at the bottom of a chord (G-C-E). Notated: $C^{(2)}$

third.......... The seventh of a chord (the note B♭ in a C7 chord) is at the bottom of a chord (B♭-C-E-G). Notated: $C7^{(3)}$

fourth .... When the ninth of a chord (the note D in a C9 chord) is at the bottom of a chord (D-E-G-B♭-C). Notated: $C9^{(4)}$

Root Position .... When a chord is written line-line-line (line-line) or space-space-space (space-space), it is in root position. The root is the bottom note.

Split Chords.. Chords which contain a bass note which is not the root of the chord. Often the bass note is not a note from the chord at all.

major 7 ...... Puts a maj7 chord in the right hand (C-E-G-B) over a bass note in the left hand, usually down at least one octave, other than the root (D). Notated: Cmaj7/D

minor 7 ...... Puts a m7 chord in the right hand (C-E♭-G-B♭) over a bass note in the left hand, usually down at least one octave, other than the root (B♭). Notated: Cm7/B♭

major 6 ...... Combines a maj6 chord in the right hand (C-E-G-A) over a bass note in the left hand, usually down at least one octave, other than the root (D). Notated: C6/D

Sus4 Chords.. Also known as a "sus" chord. When a triad is written using the fourth degree of the scale instead of the third, the fourth is said to be "suspending" the expected resolution to the third.

7sus .... Raises the third of a 7 chord to the fourth (C-F-G-B♭). Notated: C7sus

Melodic Structures

Blues scale.... A six-note blues scale consists of a minor pentatonic scale with the addition of a flatted fifth (or sharpened fourth) scale degree (C-E♭-F-G♭-G-B♭).

Modes .... Scales with names drawn from the ancient Greeks, used in folk, pop, and some classical pieces.

Dorian .... A seven-note scale with half steps between scale degrees 2-3 and 6-7 (C-D-E♭-F-G-A-B♭-C).

Lydian .... A seven-note scale with half steps between scale degrees 4-5 and 7-8 (C-D-E-F♯-G-A-B-C).

Mixolydian.. A seven-note scale with half steps between scale degrees 3-4 and 6-7 (C-D-E-F-G-A-B♭-C).

Phrygian..... A seven-note scale with half steps between scale degrees 1-2 and 5-6 (C-D♭-E♭-F-G-A♭-B♭-C).

Pentatonic .... A five-note scale based on the first five notes of the overtone series (C-G-D-A-E), arranged in scale form (C-D-E-G-A).

major......... A common form of this five-note scale uses scale degrees 1-2-3-5-6 of a major scale (C-D-E-G-A).

minor .... A common form of this five-note scale uses scale degrees 1-3-4-5-7 of a natural minor scale (C-E♭-F-G-B♭).

Terms & Symbols

Licks........... Short, catchy melodic motifs, often used to describe guitar playing.

Motif .... A group of notes that form a musical idea.

Ostinato....... A rhythmic or melodic pattern repeated at length in one voice.

Repeat

full bar....... Repeat the entire previous measure.

double full bar .... repeat the entire previous two measures.

Riff............. Another term for ostinato, often used in pop music. A repeated pattern of notes, chord progression, or rhythmic pattern, often played by the rhythm section.

Slash notation........... Signals performers to create their own rhythmic pattern. A slash is placed over each beat.

Tremolo .... A fast alternation between two notes, notated by strokes on the stem of the notes, or between the stems of the notes.